COLLINS
COBUILD

ENGLISH
GUIDES
6: HOMOPHONES

THE UNIVERSITY
OF BIRMINGHAM

COLLINS
COBUILD

HarperCollins*Publishers*

HarperCollins Publishers
77-85 Fulham Palace Road
London W6 8JB

COBUILD is a trademark of William Collins Sons & Co Ltd

© HarperCollins Publishers Ltd 1995
First published 1995

10 9 8 7 6 5 4 3 2 1

ISBN 0 00 370565 X

Computer typeset by Tradespools Ltd, Frome, Somerset

Printed in Great Britain by HarperCollins Manufacturing, Glasgow

Corpus Acknowledgements

We would like to acknowledge the assistance of the many hundreds of
individuals and companies who have kindly given permission for
copyright material to be used in The Bank of English. The written
sources include many national and regional newspapers in Britain and
overseas; magazine and periodical publishers; and book publishers in
Britain, the United States, and Australia. Extensive spoken data has
been provided by radio and television broadcasting companies; research
workers at many universities and other institutions; and numerous
individual contributors. We are grateful to them all.

The COBUILD Series

Founding Editor–in–Chief   John Sinclair

Editorial Team

Editorial Director   Gwyneth Fox

Series Editor   Jane Bradbury

Editors   Helen Bruce
Mike Stocks

Computer Staff   Tim Lane
Andrea Lewis

Secretarial Staff   Sue Crawley
Michelle Devereux

HarperCollins *Publishers*

Gillian McNair

Acknowledgements

We would like to thank Annette Capel for her invaluable contribution to the early stages of this project and Susan Hunston for her helpful comments on the text.

Foreword

The *Guide to Homophones* is one of a series of COBUILD ENGLISH GUIDES to particular areas of special interest to learners of English.

Homophones, or words such as 'pair' and 'pear' which sound the same but are spelled differently, can be a problem for learners of English for two main reasons: the first is that they can cause confusion when writing; the second is that the different spellings can be difficult to find in a dictionary, as it is not easy to guess how a word is spelled, and this makes it difficult for learners to establish which word is which. By putting groups of homophones together with a clear explanation of what they mean, and with real examples to show how they are used, this Guide allows learners to learn and remember the different spellings and meanings so that they can write more accurately, and can increase their vocabulary and understanding of different spelling patterns. Teachers can use this Guide as the basis for lessons or exercises based on building vocabulary and improving spelling by asking students to distinguish between homophones, for example by putting them in sentences to show how they are used, or by setting questions such as 'which would you wring, a bell or a wet cloth?', which would encourage students to look at the difference between 'wring' and 'ring'.

This book, like all COBUILD books, is derived from studying the evidence in The Bank of English, which contains over 200 million words. The examples are taken directly from the corpus and the frequency of words affects the prominence given to them here.

We hope that you find this book helpful and easy to use. Please write to us with any comments or suggestions about how to improve COBUILD publications.

Gwyneth Fox
Editorial Director
COBUILD

Introduction

Homophones are words which sound the same but are spelt differently. For example, *pair* and *pear* are homophones. These words can cause problems for students when they are writing English, as they may not know which spelling is correct. They can also cause problems when students are trying to understand spoken English—imagine hearing the sentence 'put the dough in the oven for two hours' if you do not know how to spell 'dough'. You might look up an obvious spelling and find 'doe', which would not explain the sentence at all, and there would be nothing to indicate that there is in fact another word which sounds exactly the same but has a very different meaning.

This book is intended to help you to increase your vocabulary and improve your spelling. By arranging homophones together in groups with a clear explanation of the main meanings of the words and plenty of examples to show how they are used, this book helps you to learn the differences between these words so that you can understand and use them properly.

To use homophones correctly, the most important things you need to know about are spelling and meaning, and these are the areas that are focused on. Helpful grammar information is also given, but if you would like a more detailed explanation of the grammar of a particular word, you should look at a dictionary such as the COBUILD English Dictionary.

Where a word is very common indeed, such as **the** or **for**, only a very simple explanation is given, as it is likely that you already know the main uses of this word. Where a word has a large number of meanings, the entry focuses on the most common ones, to give you a clear idea of the main uses of that word.

This book looks at over three hundred of the most common groups of homophones in English, covering over seven hundred different words. We believe that using this book will help you to increase your confidence in writing and understanding English, and we hope that it will prove a useful aid to increasing your vocabulary and improving your spelling.

How to use this book

The ordering of entries

The book contains groups of homophones arranged alphabetically according to which of the words in that group is explained first. In most cases, this is the word that occurs most frequently, but in a few cases where the frequency of the words is almost the same, the word which occurs first alphabetically is given first. So, for example, the first entry in this book is **add, ad**, because **add** is a more frequently used word than **ad**, and the second entry is **aid, aide**, because **aid** is a more frequently used word than **aide**. It is likely that you will be familiar with the more commonly used words, and so you will probably already know how to spell them.

The entries
The groups of homophones

Each entry begins with the homophones, arranged in one of the ways explained above, shown next to information on how these words are pronounced. A full explanation of the pronunciation system used in this book is given on page xii.

After each word in the group is a list of its inflected forms, showing you which of these are also homophones. For example, if you look at the first entry, **add, ad**, you will see that **adds** and **ads** are in bold because they are homophones too, and *adding* and *added* are not in bold because they are not homophones.

Sometimes, inflected forms also appear in another entry, and when this is the case there is a cross reference so that you know where else to look. For example, at the entry for **ball, bawl**, there is a cross reference to the entry for **bald, bawled**, as **bawled** is one of the inflected forms of **bawl**.

The explanations of the words in the group

Next, there is an explanation of the uses of the first word in the group, which includes information on grammar and a number of real examples to show how the word is used.

This is followed by an explanation of the most common uses of the second word in the group, again with information on grammar and some examples, and so on until all the homophones have been explained.

In the explanation of each use of each word, the key word appears in **bold**. Sometimes, other words also appear in **bold**. This is to show that the word being explained is always used in the way shown.

A full explanation of the grammatical terms used in this book is given on pages vii–xi.

How to find a word in this book

Sometimes, one of the words in a group of homophones is an inflected form of another word:

● When this other word occurs in another entry in this book, rather than explaining it again, there is a cross reference to the entry where it is explained. For example, at the entry for **bearer, barer**, the explanation of **bearer** tells you that it is the comparative form of **bear**, and that you should look at the entry for **bear, bare** for an explanation of the uses of **bear**.

● When this other word does not occur in another entry in this book, an explanation of its uses is given, along with a note telling you which word it is an inflected form of. For example, at the entry for **allowed, aloud**, the explanation of **allowed** begins by saying that it is the '-ed' form of the verb 'allow', and then goes on to explain the uses of this verb.

As the entries are arranged alphabetically according to the first word in a group of homophones, it may not always be clear to you where to look for a word. To help you, there is an index at the back of the book telling you where to find each of the individual words covered by this book.

Understanding the grammar information in this book

Verb

A **verb** is a word such as 'sing', 'eat', or 'make' which is used with a subject to say what someone or something does or what happens to them, or to give information about them.

This book does not give detailed information about how verbs are used. If you want to know more about a particular verb, look at the entry for it in a dictionary such as the COBUILD English Dictionary.

Phrasal Verb

A **phrasal verb** is a combination of a verb and an adverb or preposition, for example, 'get up' or 'look after', which together have a particular meaning.

Noun

A **noun** is a word such as 'teacher', 'cat', 'knife', or 'happiness' which is used to refer to a person or thing. Below is an explanation of the main types of noun and how they are used.

● count noun

A **count noun** has a plural form, usually made by adding 's'. When it is singular, it must have a determiner in front of it such as 'a', 'her', or 'such'. *My mum used to take me to the fair there...clothes strewn all over the floor*.

● uncount noun

An **uncount noun** refers to things that are not normally counted or considered to be individual items. Uncount nouns do not have a plural form, and are used with a singular verb. They do not need determiners. *The creature's fur is short, dense, and silky...the smell of cooking filled the air*.

● singular noun

A **singular noun** is always singular, and needs a determiner. *The hail didn't come as predicted...After a certain lapse of time, it would be safe for Daisy to return*.

● plural noun

A **plural noun** is always plural, and is used with plural verbs. If a

pronoun is used to stand for the noun, it is a plural pronoun such as 'they' or 'them'. *I think we should all strive to have good manners* ... *Sales of Japanese cars have risen by nearly ten per cent.*
Plural nouns which end in 's' often lose the 's' when they come in front of another noun, for example, *stairs, stair carpet*. If they refer to a single object which has two main parts, such as 'jeans' or 'glasses', the expression 'a pair of' is sometimes used: *a pair of jeans, a pair of glasses*.

● mass noun

A **mass noun** typically combines the behaviour of both count and uncount nouns in the same sense. It is used like an uncount noun to refer to a substance. It is used like a count noun to refer to a brand or type. *Combine the flour with 3 tablespoons of water...Most bakers use the same blend of flours*.

● variable noun

A **variable noun** typically combines the behaviour of both count and uncount nouns in the same sense. The singular form occurs freely both with and without determiners. Variable nouns also have a plural form, usually made by adding 's'. Some variable nouns when used like uncount nouns refer to abstract things like 'hardship' and 'injustice', and when used as count nouns refer to individual examples or instances of that thing. *He is not afraid to protest against injustice...It is never too late to correct an injustice...the injustices of world poverty*. Others refer to objects which can be mentioned either individually or generally, like 'potato': you can talk about 'a potato', 'potatoes', or 'potato'.

● proper noun

A **proper noun** refers to one person, place, thing, or institution, and begins with a capital letter. Many proper nouns are used without a determiner, for example *I am going to America*, and some must be used with 'the', for example *the Ice Age*.

● collective count noun, collective uncount noun

A **collective count noun** refers to a group of people or things. It behaves like a count noun, but when it is in the singular form it can be used with either a singular or a plural verb. *The audience are much younger than average...The British audience has a huge appetite for serials...Audiences are becoming more selective*.

A **collective uncount noun** refers to a group of people or things. It behaves like an uncount noun, but can be used with either a singular or a plural verb. *....in a country where livestock outnumber people ten to one...Any kind of livestock is totally dependent on its owner for all its needs*.

Pronoun

A **pronoun** is a word which you use to refer to someone or something when you do not need or want to use a noun, often because the person or thing has been mentioned earlier. Examples of pronouns are 'it', 'she', 'something', and 'myself'.

Adjective

An **adjective** is a word such as 'big', 'healthy', or 'economical' that describes a person or thing, or gives extra information about them. Adjectives usually come before nouns or after link verbs.

Adverb

An **adverb** is a word such as 'slowly', 'now', 'very', 'politically', or 'fortunately' which adds information about the action, event, or situation mentioned in a clause.

Determiner

A **determiner** is a word which is used at the beginning of a noun group to indicate, for example, which thing you are referring to or whether you are referring to one thing or several. Common English determiners are 'a', 'the', 'some', 'this', and 'each'.

Quantifier

A **quantifier** is a word or phrase like 'plenty' or 'a lot' which allows you to refer to the quantity of something without being absolutely precise. They are followed by 'of' and a noun group, for example _a lot of money_.

Preposition

A **preposition** is a word such as 'by', 'for', 'into', or 'with' which is always followed by a noun group or the '-ing' form of a verb.

Conjunction

A **conjunction** is a word or a group of words that joins together words, groups, or clauses. In English there are co-ordinating conjunctions, such as 'and' and 'but', and subordinating conjunctions such as 'although', 'because', and 'when'.

Title

A **title** is used to refer to someone who has a particular role or position. Titles come before the name of a person and begin with a capital letter, for example _Father Subev_, _Lord Lane_.

Titles can sometimes be used to refer to people who have a particular role or position, for example *He became a Lord in 1976.*

Number

A **number** is a word such as 'four' or 'eight'. Numbers such as 'one', 'two', or 'three' are used like determiners, for example *three bears;* like adjectives, for example *the four horsemen;* like pronouns, for example *She has three cases and I have two;* and like quantifiers, for example *Six of the boys stayed behind.*

Numbers such as 'hundred', 'thousand', and 'million' always follow a determiner or another number, for example *two hundred bears...the hundred horsemen...She has a thousand dollars and I have a million...A hundred of the boys stayed behind.*

Colour

A **colour** word refers to a colour. It is like an adjective, for example *...the blue sky...The sky is blue;* and also like a noun, for example *She was dressed in red...different shades of green.*

Phrase

A **phrase** is a small group of words which forms a unit, either on its own or within a sentence.

Convention

A **convention** is a word or a fixed phrase which is used in conversation, for example when you are greeting someone, apologizing, or replying.

Vocative

A **vocative** is used when speaking directly to someone or writing to them. Vocatives do not need a determiner, but some may be used with a possessive determiner. *I'm sure they will take good care of you, dear...How are you, my dear?*

'-s' form

The **'-s' form** of a verb is the third person singular form of that verb. It is used in the present tense with subjects such as 'the girl', 'he', and 'it', and is usually formed by adding 's' to the base form of the verb. For example, 'adds' is the '-s' form of 'add'; 'drives' is the '-s' form of 'drive'.

'-ed' form

The **'-ed' form** of a verb is the past tense and past participle of that verb. It is usually formed by adding 'ed' to the end of the base form of the verb, but if the verb ends in 'e', the 'e' is dropped, and if the verb ends in 'y', the 'y' is usually changed to 'i'. For example 'posted' is the '-ed' form of 'post'; 'carried' is the '-ed' form of carry; 'hated' is the '-ed' form of 'hate'.

'-ing' form

The **'-ing' form** of a verb is the present participle of that verb. Present participles are used with auxiliary verbs to make continuous tenses. They are also used like adjectives, describing a person or thing as doing something. They are usually formed by adding 'ing' to the base form of the verb, but if the verb ends in 'e' the 'e' is usually dropped. For example, 'walking' is the '-ing' form of walk; 'hurrying' is the '-ing' form of 'hurry'; 'leaving' is the '-ing' form of 'leave'.

Pronunciation

Information on pronunciation is an important part of this book, and our aim has been to provide a pronunciation key that is accurate, clear, and simple.

The transcription system, explained below, has developed from the original work by Dr David Brazil for the Collins COBUILD English Language Dictionary. The symbols used in this book are adapted from those of the International Phonetic Alphabet (**IPA**).

IPA symbols

Vowel Sounds

ɑː	calm, ah	ɒ	lot, spot
ɑːʳ	heart, far	oʊ	note, coat
æ	act, mass	ɔː	claw, faun
aɪ	dive, cry	ɔʳ	more, cord
aɪəʳ	fire, tyre	ɔɪ	boy, joint
aʊ	out, down	ʊ	could, stood
aʊəʳ	flour, sour	uː	you, use
e	met, lend, pen	ʊəʳ	lure, pure
eɪ	say, weight	ɜːʳ	turn, third
eəʳ	fair, care	ʌ	fund, must
ɪ	fit, win	ə	the first vowel in about
iː	feed, me	əʳ	the first vowel in forgotten
ɪəʳ	near, beard	i	the second vowel in very
		u	the second vowel in actual

Consonant Sounds

b	bed, rub	s	soon, bus
d	done, red	t	talk, bet
f	fit, if	v	van, love
g	good, dog	w	win, wool
h	hat, horse	ʰw	why, wheat
j	yellow, you	x	loch
k	pick, kick	z	zoo, buzz
l	lip, bill	ʃ	ship, wish
ᵊl	handle, panel	ʒ	measure, leisure
m	mat, ram	ŋ	sing, working
n	not, tin	tʃ	cheap, witch
ᵊn	hidden, written	θ	thin, myth
p	pay, lip	ð	then, bathe
r	run, read	dʒ	joy, bridge

add, adds, adding, added
ad, ads
/æd/

add

VERB

Add is a frequently used verb with a number of meanings, all of which have to do with putting things together. For example, if you **add** two numbers, you put them together in order to calculate their total; if you **add** something when you are speaking, you say something more.

Give your child a list of numbers to add.
That's something else to add to my worries.
Any further delay would add billions to the cost.
'It's not so easy finding friends in a small town,' he adds.

● **Add** also occurs in following phrasal verbs: **add up; add up to.**

ad

COUNT NOUN

An **ad** is an advertisement; an informal word.

Someone saw the ad and called to report he had found the dog.
Burnett is America's 13th-biggest ad agency.

aid, aids, aiding, aided
aide, aides
/eɪd/

aid

UNCOUNT NOUN

Aid is money, equipment, or services provided for people in need.

...hundreds of thousands of tons of food aid arriving from Western countries and charitable organizations.
...the withdrawal of foreign forces and the cessation of military aid.

COUNT NOUN

An **aid** is something that makes a particular thing easier to do. When **aid** is used in this way, it is usually modified.

She adjusted the power on her hearing aid.

VERB

To **aid** a person or organization means to help them.

The president has been criticized for failing to aid minority groups.

1

The United States, which aids the rebels, has stepped up its efforts to end the conflict.

UNCOUNT NOUN

AIDS is an illness which destroys the body's natural system of protection against diseases.

Jon died of AIDS in 1982.

aide

COUNT NOUN

An **aide** is an assistant to a person who has an important job.

...the President's former aide.

---

air, airs
heir, heirs
ere

/ɛəʳ/

---

air

UNCOUNT NOUN

Air is the space and gases around and above us.

She opened the door and the smell of cooking filled the air.
...air pollution.

UNCOUNT NOUN

Air is used in expressions such as 'by air' to refer to travel in aircraft.

About twenty thousand Sri Lankans have already been repatriated by air since the crisis began.

SINGULAR NOUN

If someone or something has a particular **air**, they give that general impression.

There was an air of gloom and despair hanging over us.
For all its unshowy and unfussy air, this is an impressive little book.

PLURAL NOUN

Airs are exaggerated or unnatural manners.

The family was an old one and apparently gave itself airs.

heir

COUNT NOUN

Someone's **heir** is the person who will inherit their money or property.

Tilda seems to be his only heir.
His heirs were forced to sell the house.

ere

Ere means 'before': a literary word.

*But it was not long ere a call came from the house and recalled me
from my reflections.*

---

ale, ales
ail, ails, ailing, ailed

/e͟ɪl/

---

ale

MASS NOUN

Ale is a kind of beer.

...luke-warm bottled ale.

ail

VERB

To **ail** means to be ill; an old-fashioned word.

*Just what ails Herr Honecker will be ascertained in a preliminary
health check in Berlin.*

VERB

If something **ails** a country or an organization, it is a problem or a
source of difficulty for that country or organization; a formal use.

It may provide answers to some of the problems that ail America.

---

allowed
aloud

/əla͟ʊd/

---

allowed

Allowed is the '-ed' form of the verb 'allow'.

VERB

If something **is allowed**, it is permitted.

Smoking is not allowed in the dining room.
Obviously this situation must not be allowed to go on much longer.

aloud

ADVERB

If you say something **aloud,** you say it so that other people can hear you.

She was tempted to make this comment aloud, but restrained herself.
The expression of sheer joy on her face made him laugh aloud.

---

alter, alters, altering, altered
altar, altars

/ˈɔːltər/

---

alter

VERB

To **alter** something means to change it.

Global warming is going to alter the nature of the climate.
There are few signs that either side is ready to alter its position.

altar

COUNT NOUN

An **altar** is a holy table in a Christian church.
The church was in darkness except for the altar.

---

arc, arcs
Ark

/ˈɑːrk/

---

arc

COUNT NOUN

An **arc** is a curve.
If you throw a ball, it does not move in a straight line but in an arc.

Ark

PROPER NOUN

In the Bible, the **Ark** was a large wooden boat used by Noah to save his family and two of every kind of animal from the flood.

arms
alms
/ˈɑːmz/

arms

Arms is the plural form of the noun 'arm'.

COUNT NOUN

Your **arms** are your two upper limbs.
His nose and one of his arms were broken.

PLURAL NOUN

Arms are weapons that are used in a war.
They have so far restricted their military support to small arms, anti-tank weapons, mortar, and ammunition.

alms

PLURAL NOUN

Alms are gifts of food, money, or clothes for poor people; an old-fashioned word.
The neighbourhood was noisy, beggars asked for alms, and drunks slept in the doorways.

---

ascent, ascents
assent, assents, assenting, assented
/əˈsent/

ascent

COUNT NOUN

An **ascent** is a movement from a low level to a higher level.
...an ascent of the treacherous K2 mountain in the Himalayas.

assent

UNCOUNT NOUN

If someone gives their **assent** to something that has been suggested, they agree to it.
She was thoughtful for a moment, then nodded her head in assent.
In Scotland 16 and 17 year-olds do not need parental assent to get married.

VERB

To **assent** to something means to agree to it.
He had no choice but to assent to the signing of the document.
When I explain he assents, but dubiously.

---

bail,
bale, bales

/beɪl/

---

bail

UNCOUNT NOUN

If someone who has been accused of a crime is granted **bail**, they are given permission to be released until their trial.

An application for bail was refused.
They were released on £2,600 bail.

● **Bale** also occurs in the phrasal verb **bail out**, which can also be spelt 'bale out'.

bale

COUNT NOUN

A **bale** of something is a bundle of it.

...a bale of hay.
Almost four billion bales of wool remain unsold.

---

bald, balder, baldest
bawled

/bɔːld/

---

bald

ADJECTIVE

Someone who is **bald** has little or no hair on the top of his or her head.

...a fat bald man.
He was prominently visible because of his bald head.

ADJECTIVE

A **bald** statement, question, or account has no unnecessary words or details in it.

Behind these bald words there lies a tale of bitter jealousy and rivalry.

bawled

VERB

Bawled is the '-ed' form of the verb 'bawl'. See **ball, bawl** for an explanation of the uses of this word.

Later that same day a left-wing Labour MP bawled abuse in the face of a minister.
'This is a good place to exchange ideas,' he bawled unconvincingly above the din.

ball, balls
bawl, bawls, bawling, bawled

/bɔːl/

See also **bald, bawled**.

ball

COUNT NOUN

A **ball** is a round object.

Mortenson noticed some lads kicking a ball about on the sands.
...a ball of wool.
Divide the mixture into twelve balls.

COUNT NOUN

A **ball** is a formal social event with dancing.

The office staff received an invitation to a charity ball.

bawl

VERB

To **bawl** means to shout or cry loudly.

They took it in turns to bawl abuse at their opponents.
The children continued to bawl.

● **Bawl** also occurs in the phrasal verb **bawl out**.

band, bands
banned

/bænd/

band

COUNT NOUN

A **band** is a group of musicians.

She sang in a series of concerts with the Basie Band.

COUNT NOUN

A **band** of people is a group of people who share the same beliefs about something.

...the apparently growing band of US critics.
From then until 1 am the Prime Minister and a band of his intimates worked almost non-stop.

COUNT NOUN

A **band** of numbers or values is a range of numbers or values.

The government issued figures last year for the proportion of properties it believed would fall into each band.

banned

Banned is the '-ed' form of the verb 'ban'.

VERB

If an organization or activity **is banned**, it is officially forbidden.

...a suggestion that future demonstrations might be banned.
...the leaders of the banned political parties.

---

bans
banns   /bænz/

---

bans

Bans is the '-s' form of the verb 'ban' and the plural form of the noun 'ban'.

COUNT NOUN

Bans are official statements forbidding something.

Several water companies have imposed hosepipe bans.

VERB

If someone **bans** something, they officially prevent or forbid it.

...a law which bans discrimination against the handicapped not only in employment but also in other areas of life.

banns

PLURAL NOUN

When a vicar reads or publishes the **banns**, he makes a public announcement in church that a man and a woman are going to get married.

If the bride and groom live in different parishes, banns must be read in both.

---

barmy, barmier, barmiest
balmy, balmier, balmiest   /bɑːmi/

---

barmy

ADJECTIVE

If you describe someone as **barmy**, you mean that they are slightly mad or foolish; an informal word.

Most of his friends think he's barmy.

It seems that football fans are even barmier than we thought.

balmy

ADJECTIVE

Balmy weather is mild and pleasant.

...*a balmy spring day in the capital.*

---

baron, barons
barren

/bærən/

---

baron

COUNT NOUN

A **baron** is a male member of the British nobility.

Jack Ashley took his seat in the House of Lords as Baron Ashley of Stoke.

COUNT NOUN

You can use **baron** to refer to a person who controls a large part of an organization or industry. When **baron** is used in this way, it is usually modified.

His record as a newspaper baron is not at all bad.
...*the killing of a suspected drugs baron.*

barren

ADJECTIVE

Barren land has poor soil and crops cannot be produced on it.

The once-fertile earth has become parched and barren.
...*the cluster of barren, almost uninhabited islands.*

ADJECTIVE

A **barren** woman cannot have children; an old-fashioned use.

Barren women are rejected by the tribesmen.

ADJECTIVE

A **barren** period of time is empty or unproductive.

...*the barren, wasted five years of exile.*

base, bases, basing, based
bass, basses

/be͟ɪs/

base

COUNT NOUN

The **base** of something is the lowest edge or part of it.

It has pale pink flowers flushed with a glowing yellow at their base.
...the heavy base of the gun.

COUNT NOUN

A **base** is a thing used to develop or achieve something else. When **base** is used in this way, it is usually modified.

His priorities include establishing a stronger financial and administrative base for their work.

COUNT NOUN

Someone's **base** is the main place where they work, stay, or live.

The hotel is a perfect base for us.
Several army bases have come under fire.

VERB

If you **base** one thing **on** another, you develop the general form, subject, or nature of the first thing from the second thing.

The intention is to base any help on the facilities that exist already.
...a valuable document on which to base future decisions.

bass

COUNT NOUN

A **bass** is a man with a deep singing voice.

...the bass who sang the role of Boris Godunov at Covent Garden.

ADJECTIVE

A **bass** musical instrument has a low-pitch.

...the electric bass guitar.

Note that **bass** can also be pronounced /ba͟es/, and that it has a different meaning when it is pronounced in this way; a **bass** is a type of fish.

bays
baize   /be͟ɪz/

bays

Bays is the plural form of the noun 'bay'.

COUNT NOUN

Bays are parts of the coastline where the land curves inwards.
From the bays the local community gathered molluscs and shellfish.

COUNT NOUN

Bays are spaces or areas used for a particular purpose.
...cars parked illegally at meters or in residents' parking bays.
...a ward with six bays for beds and a nurse's station in one corner.

baize

UNCOUNT NOUN

Baize is a thick green woollen material used for covering snooker tables and card tables.
...a large green baize table.

be
bee   /bi͟ː/

be

Note that **be** can also be pronounced /bi/. It is pronounced /bi͟ː/ at the end of a sentence or when you want to emphasize it (this is known as the strong form), and /bi/ in all other cases (this is known as the weak form).

VERB

Be is a frequently used verb. You are probably familiar with the uses shown in the examples below. Look in a COBUILD dictionary if you need a fuller explanation of the uses of this word.

It is not going to be easy.
This will be a slow, tough process.
I should be at work, actually.

bee

COUNT NOUN

A **bee** is a striped insect which makes honey.
I got stung by a bee last night.

---

beach, beaches
beech, beeches
/biːtʃ/

---

beach

COUNT NOUN

A **beach** is an area of sand or pebbles by the edge of the sea.

...*miles of sandy and rocky beaches.*

beech

VARIABLE NOUN

A **beech** is a type of tree.

...*broadleaved trees such as beech and oak.*

---

bear, bears, bearing, bore, borne
bare, bares, baring, bared; barer, barest
/beəʳ/

See also **bearing, baring; bore, boar; born, borne; bearer, barer.**

bear

COUNT NOUN

A **bear** is a large, strong wild animal with thick fur and sharp claws.

He was killed by a bear.

VERB

If you say that you cannot **bear** an unpleasant or difficult situation, you mean that you are not able to accept it or deal with it mentally.

Joan simply cannot bear the thought of her little grandson being blind for the rest of his life.
Macleod bears his sorrows with dignity.

VERB

To **bear** something means to carry, support, or bring it.

It is vital to make sure your balcony will bear the weight of plants and containers.
A small child approached them bearing a net bag.

VERB

To **bear** a particular mark or characteristic means to have that mark or characteristic.

Her wrists still bear the marks of cigarette burns.
...a strip of paper bearing his name.

VERB

If a woman **bears** a child, she gives birth to it.

He married her because she was about to bear his child.

● **Bear** also occurs in the following phrasal verbs: **bear down; bear out; bear up; bear with.**

bare

ADJECTIVE

If someone's body or a part of their body is **bare**, it is naked.

Faces and bare bodies were scorched red by the sun.
...a little girl with bare legs.

ADJECTIVE

Something that is **bare** is empty or uncovered.

The fridge was bare but for a rind of cheese.
The trees were almost bare.

VERB

To **bare** something means to uncover it.

She may never bare her body on screen again.
Wolves with burning eyes gathered around him, baring their teeth as they snarled and howled.

---

bearer, bearers
barer

/ˈbeərəʳ/

---

bearer

COUNT NOUN

The **bearer** of a particular thing is the person who carries or brings it; a literary word.

He might be the bearer of more food.
It's not easy to be the bearer of unwelcome news.

barer

ADJECTIVE

Barer is the comparative form of the adjective 'bare'. See **bear, bare** for an explanation of the uses of this word.

The shelves of Moscow grocery shops are becoming barer and barer.

13

bearing
baring

/ˈbeərɪŋ/

bearing

VERB

Bearing is the '-ing' form of the verb **bear**. See **bear, bare** for examples and an explanation of the uses of this verb.

PHRASE

If something **has some bearing** on a certain event, it has some effect on it or some connection with it.

This crisis and its effect in raising petrol prices has some bearing on the main story in the press.
That complication has no bearing on the present issue.

SINGULAR NOUN

A person's **bearing** is the way in which they move or stand.

...his tall, slightly stooped and distinguished bearing.

baring

VERB

Baring is the '-ing' form of the verb 'bare'. See **bear, bare** for examples and an explanation of the uses of this word.

beat, beats, beating, beaten
beet

/biːt/

beat

Note that the form **beat** is used in the present tense and is also the past tense form of the verb.

VERB

To **beat** someone means to hit them very hard repeatedly.

Death squads have shot hundreds of children and routinely beat and tortured others.
She dug her nails into my face and scratched and beat me.

VERB

To **beat** someone in a game or competition means to defeat them or do better than them.

In today's semi-finals, Graf beat Lindquist in straight sets.
They beat Crystal Palace one-nil in a replay at Wembley.

COUNT NOUN

The **beat** of a piece of music is the main rhythm that it has.

The beat is rapid and mesmerising.

● **Beat** also occurs in the following phrasal verbs: **beat down; beat up.**

beet

UNCOUNT NOUN

Beet is a type of vegetable.

...the acres of wheat or sugar beet.

---

bell, bells
belle, belles

/b**e**l/

---

bell

COUNT NOUN

A **bell** is a device or object that makes a ringing sound.

He had waited for some time before ringing the door bell.
A deep bell was ringing a funeral toll.

belle

COUNT NOUN

A **belle** is a beautiful woman; an old-fashioned word, used in American English.

...Eleanor Poindexter, a belle from Baltimore.

---

birth, births
berth, berths, berthing, berthed

/b**ɜːʳ**θ/

---

birth

COUNT NOUN

When a baby is born, you refer to this event as its **birth**.

The birth of her second child brought her career to a temporary halt.
...the 235th anniversary of the composer's birth.

berth

PHRASE

If you **give** someone or something **a wide berth**, you avoid them because you think that they are unpleasant or dangerous.

The terrorists give government forces a wide berth.

15

VERB

When ships **berth**, they arrive at a harbour and stop at a quay.

The first passenger ship has been delayed and is now scheduled to berth at four hours GMT on Sunday.

COUNT NOUN

A **berth** is a space for a boat in a harbour.

All four boats in berths 5 and 6 were deserted.

COUNT NOUN

A **berth** is a bed in a boat, train, or caravan.

The ship has berths for 750 passengers.

---

bite, bites, biting, bit
byte, bytes

/b**aɪ**t/

---

bite

VERB

To **bite** something means to cut or make a hole in it with your teeth.

Before she could turn round he tried to bite her.
When a question bothers her, she bites the knuckles of her hands.

COUNT NOUN

A **bite** is a cut or small hole made in something using your teeth.

...a bite from a dog.
...an adder bite.
Many illnesses are passed on through insect bites.

VERB

When something such as an action, law, or policy starts to **bite**, it starts to have a noticeable effect, usually one that people find unpleasant.

The economic blockade is beginning to bite.
Whenever a recession bites, the list of casualties is dramatic.

byte

COUNT NOUN

A **byte** is a unit of storage in a computer.

The machine's magnetic drum stored a mere 300 bytes.

block, blocks, blocking, blocked

bloc, blocs

/bl<u>o</u>k/

block

COUNT NOUN

A **block** of something is a square or rectangular piece of it.

...*a block of marble.*

COUNT NOUN

A **block** is a large building. When **block** is used in this way, it is usually modified.

...*a block of flats.*

COUNT NOUN

A **block** is an area in a town surrounded by streets; used mainly in American English.

Shabby brick apartments stretch for block after block.

VERB

To **block** a road, channel, or pipe means to put something across it so that nothing can get through it.

The riot police kept well out of the way except to block the road leading to sensitive government buildings.
There's concern that plastics in refuse tips may block drainage and gas flow.

VERB

To **block** something means to stop it from happening.

Mediocre managers may block the promotion of the best young people reporting to them.
He said only one obstacle now blocks the signing of a comprehensive peace settlement.

● **Block** also occurs in the following phrasal verbs: **block out; block up.**

bloc

COUNT NOUN

A **bloc** is a group of countries, organizations, or people with shared aims. When **bloc** is used in this way, it is usually modified.

...*the newly independent Eastern bloc countries.*
...*the competing power blocs inside the ruling party.*

17

---

blue, bluer, bluest
blew   /bl<u>u:</u>/

---

blue

COLOUR

Blue is the colour of the sky on a sunny day.

...a man with very blue eyes.
Rachel is dressed in blue.

ADJECTIVE

If you feel **blue**, you feel very sad; used in informal English.

He was feeling blue and lonely.

ADJECTIVE

Blue films or jokes are concerned with sex in a way that many
people find offensive or unacceptable; used in informal English.

There were some very blue jokes, I remember.

blew

Blew is the past tense form of the verb 'blow'.

VERB

The most common uses of **blew** have to do with the movement of air,
or with using a stream of air to cause an object to move or vibrate.
For example, if you say that the wind **blew**, you mean that the air
outside was moving in a way which caused objects such as trees to
move; if you say that someone **blew** a musical instrument such as a
trumpet, you mean that they used their mouth to force a stream of
air into the instrument, causing it to vibrate and make a noise.

The wind blew and shook the leaves.
A curtain of mist blew in over us.
I picked it up, blew the dust off the label, and read it.
The guard blew his whistle.
He blew his nose into a huge red handkerchief.

Blew is also used in expressions such as 'blew off' and 'blew to
pieces' to say that an object was violently removed or damaged by
the force of an explosion.

VERB

If you say that you **blew** a large amount of money **on** something, you
mean that you spent a lot of money on it, often when you did not
really need it; an informal use.

We blew twenty-three bucks on a lobster dinner.

VERB

If you fail in an attempt to do or achieve a particular thing, you can say that you **blew it**; an informal expression.

They could have been quite possibly the greatest band in the world, but they blew it because of drugs.

● **Blew** also occurs in the past tense forms of the following phrasal verbs: **blow out; blow over; blow up.**

---

bold, bolder, boldest
bowled   /bəʊld/

See also **bolder, boulder.**

bold

ADJECTIVE

Something that is **bold** is brave or daring.

Amnita becomes a bold, daring rebel.
They must take a bold decision to end the insanity.

bowled

Bowled is the '-ed' form of the verb 'bowl'.

VERB

In cricket, when the ball **is bowled**, it is thrown down the pitch towards the person who is batting.

He had bowled badly.

● **Bowled** also occurs in the '-ed' form of the following phrasal verbs: **bowl out; bowl over.**

---

bolder
boulder, boulders   /bəʊldər/

---

bolder

ADJECTIVE

Bolder is the comparative form of the adjective 'bold'. See **bold, bowled** for an explanation of the uses of this word.

The party needs to be more ambitious, bolder and less apologetic.
He seems to have taken the upper hand by making a far bolder proposition.

COUNT NOUN

A **boulder** is a large rounded rock.

I was saved from falling by a large boulder.

---

bore, bores, boring, bored

boar, boars /bɔːᵊ/

See also **bored, board**.

bore

COUNT NOUN

If you say that something is a **bore**, you mean that it is dull and you do not want to do it.

In short, the woman had become a bore.
If they turned out to be dreary bores, she could simply leave.

COUNT NOUN

A **bore** is a dull thing that you do not want to do.

Exams may appear to be a bore and even irrelevant.
What a bore!

VERB

If people or events **bore** you, you find them dull and uninteresting.

The whole business was beginning to bore him.
I don't enjoy relaxing any more; it bores me.

VERB

If you **bore** a hole in something, you make a deep round hole in it using a special tool.

Bore a hole through the woodwork and pass a brass tube through it.
The insect bores into the bark.

VERB

Bore is the past tense form of the verb 'bear'. See **bear, bare** for an explanation of the uses of this word.

She bore the anxious, unvarying monotony of the days with difficulty.
They bore the box into the kitchen and put it on the table.
He married his cousin, Hannah Hoes, who bore him four sons.

boar

COUNT NOUN

A **boar** is a pig. **Boar** is used to refer to wild pigs, or to male pigs.

A young zoology student is studying the wild boars of the Camargue.

---

bored
board, boards

/bɔːʳd/

---

bored

ADJECTIVE

If you are **bored**, you feel tired or impatient because you have lost interest in something or because you have nothing to do.

The troops overseas get very bored.
...the prospect of long summer days with bored and restless children.

VERB

Bored is the '-ed' form of the verb 'bore'. See **bore, boar** for an explanation of the uses of this word.

Most of the book had bored him, with exception of one chapter.
The prisoner bored through the wall and escaped.

board

COUNT NOUN

A **board** is a flat piece of wood.

Dice an onion on a wooden chopping board.
We had to fix a large round board like a tabletop into the wall.

COUNT NOUN

The **board** of a company or organization is the group of people who control it.

He demanded a position on the board.

VERB

To **board** a train, ship, or aircraft means to get on it.

They were arrested as they were about to board a plane for Amsterdam.

● **Board** also occurs in the phrasal verb **board up**.

---

born
borne

/bɔːʳn/

---

born

VERB

When a baby **is born**, it comes out of its mother's body at the beginning of its life. Note that this verb is only used in the passive form.

Each baby is born with its own personality and temperament.
Three years later their son James was born.

ADJECTIVE

If you say that someone is, for example, a **born** dancer or a **born** cook, you mean that they are very good at dancing or cooking and seem to have a natural talent for it.

I am a born businessman—I can't resist a deal.
He was a born scholar.

ADJECTIVE

If you say that someone is, for example, a **born** optimist or a **born** pessimist, you mean that they seem naturally to be an optimist or a pessimist and nothing that happens seems to change them.

He was a born sceptic.
...a born idealist.

borne

VERB

Borne is the past participle form of the verb 'bear'. See **bear, bare** for an explanation of the uses of this word.

I just couldn't have borne to be alone tonight.
Injured firemen were borne away in ambulances driven by volunteers.
Women who have never borne children seem to be at greater risk.

---

bow, bows, bowing, bowed
bough, boughs

/baʊ/

---

bow

VERB

To **bow** means to bend your body or head downwards.

Then she'd kneel and bow her head into her folded hands and pray.
Mumbling a prayer, he bows his head and walks on.

VERB

If you **bow to** someone's wishes, or **bow to** pressure, you agree to do something that someone wants you to do, even though you do not really want to do it.

The king was forced to bow to demands for multi-party democracy.
They will have to bow to growing public pressure and leave office.

COUNT NOUN OR PLURAL NOUN

The front part of a ship is sometimes called the **bow** or the **bows**.

Water was coming in from the bow of the boat.
The warship later tried to stop the vessel by firing across its bows.

● **Bow** also occurs in the following phrasal verbs: **bow down; bow out**.

Note that **bow** can also be pronounced /bou/, and that it has a different meaning when it is pronounced in this way; a **bow** is a knot with two loops and loose ends that is used to tie shoe laces and ribbons.

bough

COUNT NOUN

A **bough** is a large branch of a tree; a literary word.

I rested my fishing rod against a pine bough.
...jasmine scented boughs.

---

bowed
bode, bodes

/boud/

---

bowed

ADJECTIVE

Something that is **bowed** is curved.

...elegant Georgian squares and bowed crescents.

Note that **bowed** can also be pronounced /baud/, and that it has a different meaning when it is pronounced in this way; see **bow, bough**.

bode

Note that the '-ing' form and the '-ed' form of the verb 'bode' are not used.

VERB

If circumstances **bode well**, they make you think that something good is going to happen. If circumstances **bode ill**, they suggest that something bad is going to happen. 'Bode' is usually used in formal written English.

Nor does the delay bode well for the MCC, which has debt problems of its own.

All of this would bode ill for the future stability of Hong Kong.

---

boy, boys
buoy, buoys, buoying, buoyed
/bɔɪ/

---

boy

COUNT NOUN

A **boy** is a male child.

I'm married with two boys of nine and seven.

buoy

COUNT NOUN

A **buoy** is a floating object that shows boats and ships where to go.

Buoys have been placed to mark the area of the wreck.

VERB

If something **buoys** your feelings, it makes you feel more hopeful or positive.

This seemed to buoy his hopes for a political solution to the crisis.

---

bread, breads
bred
/brɛd/

---

bread

MASS NOUN

Bread is a very common food made from flour, water, and sometimes yeast.

Food markets were said to have sold out of bread and milk.

bred

Bred is the past tense form of the verb 'breed'.

VERB

Bred is used to talk about animals having babies. For example, if you say that wild animals **bred** quickly, you mean that they had a lot of babies in a short period of time; if you say that someone **bred** an animal, you mean that they owned the animal's parents and chose them carefully so that they would produce this particular animal.

The fish bred and flourished.
Three of the horses he bred became world names in show jumping.

VERB

If you say that something **bred** an unpleasant or undesirable feeling or situation, you mean that it caused that feeling or situation to develop; used mainly in formal written English.

Success has bred complacency and self-satisfaction.
...the hatred bred by three centuries of religious animosity.

---

break, breaks, breaking, broke
brake, brakes, braking, braked

/breɪk/

---

break

VERB

The most common uses of **break** have to do with damaging, destroying, or interrupting something. For example, if you **break** a glass, you damage it so that it is in several pieces and cannot be used; if you **break** your arm, you damage the bone so that it is cracked or is in several pieces.

The washing machine might break.
If the wire breaks, too much pressure was used.
He needed two operations after breaking his arm playing polo.

VERB

If you **break** a law, rule, promise, or agreement, you do something which disobeys it.

Britain had a duty to act against those who tried to break its laws.
He is widely distrusted by the voters after breaking his pledge not to raise taxes.

VERB

If you **break** the news of something to someone, usually news of something unpleasant, you tell them about it.

He breaks the bad news as gently as he can.
Police were last night breaking the news of the tragedy to her parents.

COUNT NOUN

A **break** is a period of time when you stop doing something.

...an uneventful lunch break.
My mother told me that I should take more breaks while studying.

● **Break** also occurs in the following phrasal verbs: **break in;
break into; break off; break out; break through.**

brake

COUNT NOUN

A **brake** is a device for slowing or stopping a vehicle.

The brakes were good but the car was difficult to handle.

VERB

When vehicles **brake,** they slow down or stop. When the driver of a vehicle **brakes,** he or she uses the vehicle's brakes to make it slow down or stop.

The driver at the front brakes sharply and the following vehicles pile into one another.
Suddenly he realized the truck ahead was braking, and he jammed on his brakes just in time to avoid a collision.

---

brewed
brood, broods, brooding, brooded

/bruːd/

---

brewed

Brewed is the '-ed' form of the verb 'brew'.

VERB

When drinks such as tea or beer are **brewed,** they are made.

Twenty five years ago all beer was brewed in open tanks.
...tea freshly brewed in a pot.

brood

COUNT NOUN

A **brood** of baby children or animals is a group of them belonging to the same parent.

Some kingfishers are feeding their third brood of young this summer.
...a brood of six gaily dressed children.

VERB

To **brood** about something serious or sad means to think about it a lot.

Rows happen. Don't brood on them.
Every day there is some new gloomy statistic to brood over.

---

brews
bruise, bruises, bruising, bruised

/bruːz/

---

brews

Brews is the '-s' form of the verb 'brew' and the plural form of the noun 'brew'.

COUNT NOUN

Brews are drinks such as beer or tea.

These appealing, slightly sweet brews are the staple offerings of many pubs in the area.

VERB

If someone **brews** a drink such as beer or tea, they make it.

...the company which brews lager at Northampton.

bruise

COUNT NOUN

A **bruise** is a purple mark or injury on someone's skin.

For haemophiliacs, a small cut or bruise can be life-threatening.

VERB

If you **bruise** a part of your body, you accidentally injure yourself so that a purple mark appears under your skin.

I bruise easily.

---

bridle, bridles
bridal

/braɪdᵊl/

---

bridle

COUNT NOUN

A **bridle** is a set of straps you put round a horse's head and mouth so that you can control it when you are riding it.

He retired with a broken bridle from the team contest.

VERB

To **bridle at** something means to react to it in an angry or unenthusiastic way.

Their businessmen bridle at suggestions they do business in an aggressive way.

bridal

ADJECTIVE

Bridal means related to brides or weddings.

She looked even more beautiful than usual in her bridal dress.
...the bridal suite.

---

brooch, **brooches**
broach, **broaches,** broaching, broached

/br<u>ou</u>ʃ/

---

brooch

COUNT NOUN

A **brooch** is a piece of jewellery worn on clothing.
...coral-encrusted emerald brooches.

broach

VERB

If you **broach** a difficult subject, you mention it.
The discussions continue as ministers broach the divisive question of
the size of the increase in the IMF's resources.

---

browse, browses, browsing, browsed
brows

/br<u>au</u>z/

---

browse

VERB

To **browse** means to look at things such as objects on display in a
shop or an art gallery in a casual way.
The Mosse pottery is open to visitors, who can also browse in the shop.

COUNT NOUN

A **browse** through something is a quick look at it.
A browse through the papers produces similar incongruities.
We had a quick browse around the jewellery and chocolate shops.

brows

Brows is the plural form of the noun 'brow'.

COUNT NOUN

Your **brows** are your eyebrows. Note that when **brow** is used with
this meaning, the plural form is more common than the singular.
Resemblences between them are detectable, the pale grey eyes, the
bushy brows.

COUNT NOUN

Brows can also be used to refer to people's foreheads. Note that when **brow** is used with this meaning, the singular form is more common than the plural.

Our blank eyes and furrowed brows showed that we didn't know what they were talking about.

---

build, builds, building, built

billed /bɪ̱ld/

---

build

VERB

To **build** an object or a building means to make it by joining things together.

There is now a programme to build 124 new houses.
...a joint project to build a new type of aeroplane.

VERB

To **build** an organization or society means to gradually form or develop it.

These instructions reflect Tokyo's eagerness to build a new relationship.
BZM has tried to build the kind of corporate-finance department long boasted by old-established merchant banks.

VARIABLE NOUN

Your **build** is the shape that your muscles and bones give to your body. When **build** is used in this way, it is usually modified.

He was sixty years old but his athletic build was evident even beneath his robes.

● **Build** also occurs in the following phrasal verbs: **build into; build on; build up; build upon.**

billed

Billed is the '-ed' form of the verb 'bill'.

VERB

If something **is billed as** a particular thing, it is advertised or described as being that thing.

Fo's plays are always billed as farces even though the description is false.
It had been billed as a marriage made in heaven.

burger, burgher

VERB

If someone **is billed** for goods or services they have received, they are sent a bill for those goods or services.

She has billed Mr Banks for £1,203 for publicity material.
He was billed at the standard rate.

---

burger, burgers
burgher, burghers   /bɜːʳgəʳ/

---

burger

COUNT NOUN

A **burger** is a flat, round piece of food, usually made of meat.

Children tend to choose fattier snack foods like burgers and chips.

burgher

COUNT NOUN

A **burgher** is a person who lives in a particular town; an old-fashioned word.

The local burghers have been advised to leave town.

---

bury, buries, burying, buried
berry, berries   /beri/

---

bury

VERB

To **bury** something means to put it in a hole in the ground and cover it up.

He said the authorities had been asked to bury all the bodies.
The dump buries more than a billion pounds of hazardous waste each year.

PHRASE

If you **bury** your **face in** something, you try to hide your face by pressing it against that thing.

David could see her turn and bury her face in her arms.

berry

COUNT NOUN

A **berry** is a small fruit.

Originally, Indians used roots, berries and plants for dyes.
We spent the whole afternoon berry picking.

---

bust, busts

bussed   /b<u>ʌ</u>st/

---

bust

PHRASE

If a company **goes bust**, it loses so much money that it is forced to close down.

In the mid-1980s the institute almost went bust.

COUNT NOUN

A **bust** is a statue of someone's head and shoulders.

...a bust of Lenin.

COUNT NOUN

A woman's **bust** is her breasts.

Exercise isn't going to alter the shape or size of your bust.

VERB

To **bust** something means to break it; an informal use.

It keeps coming undone—I fixed it yesterday but somebody bust it again last night.

ADJECTIVE

If something is **bust**, it is broken; an informal use.

The bed's castors are bust.

bussed

Bussed is the '-ed' form of the verb 'bus'.

VERB

If people **are bussed** somewhere, they are taken there by bus.

Tens of thousands of athletes, students and ordinary residents have been bussed in.

---

by
buy, buys, buying, bought /b<u>aɪ</u>/
bye

---

by

PREPOSITION

By is a frequently used preposition. You are probably familiar with the uses shown in the examples below. Look in a COBUILD dictionary if you need a fuller explanation of the uses of this word.

These talks were requested by Iran six weeks ago.
They are keen to avenge the deaths of their friends by catching or killing the drug dealers.
They expect to collect more money by the end of the year.
...'The Hidden Files' by Derek Raymond.
One possibility would be to ship the refugees out by boat to Italy.
The cost of child welfare services is growing by 15% a year.

buy

VERB

To **buy** something means to obtain it by paying for it.

With this sort of deal you can buy a property at a reduced price.

● **Buy** also occurs in the following phrasal verbs: **buy into; buy off; buy out; buy up;**

bye

CONVENTION

Bye is an informal way of saying goodbye.

Have a nice weekend! Bye! See you next week.

---

cannon, cannons
canon, canons /k<u>æ</u>nən/

---

cannon

COUNT NOUN

A **cannon** is a very large gun which cannot be lifted and is therefore usually on wheels or on the back of a vehicle.

The British vehicles have powerful 30mm cannons.

canon

A **canon** is one of the clergy who works in a cathedral.

...*the Reverend Canon Michael Walker.*

COUNT NOUN

A **canon** is a rule or principle on which something is based; a formal use. When **canon** is used in this way, it is usually followed by 'of'.

Internationalism is a fundamental canon of Trotskyism.
The building fulfilled none of the canons of respectable architecture.

---

canvas, canvases
canvass, canvasses, canvassing, canvassed

/kǽnvəs/

canvas

UNCOUNT NOUN

Canvas is strong heavy cloth.

He carried a canvas satchel under one arm.

VARIABLE NOUN

A **canvas** is a piece of canvas on which an oil painting is done. You can also use **canvas** to refer to the painting itself.

...*oil paintings on canvas.*
The studio was in disarray, canvases and drawings everywhere.

canvass

VERB

To **canvass** for a particular person or political party means to try to persuade people to vote for them.

Afterwards they began to canvass for support for the breakaway faction.
They offered to canvass for him.

VERB

To **canvass** opinion means to find out how people feel about something.

I suggested that the headmaster sent a questionnaire to canvass parents' views about the suitability of Saturday school.

---

carrot, carrots

carat, carats

/ˈkærət/

---

carrot

VARIABLE NOUN

A **carrot** is a long, thin orange vegetable.

Add carrots to potatoes halfway through the cooking time.

COUNT NOUN

You can refer to something that is offered to people in order to persuade them to do something as a **carrot**. The word 'stick' is often used to refer to harsher methods of persuasion.

...the juicy carrot of high profits.
The Prime Minister has decided to use the carrot as well as the stick.

carat

COUNT NOUN

A **carat** is a unit used for measuring the weight of precious stones.

Mr. Archer sells his diamonds to local jewelers for £200 a carat.

COUNT NOUN

A **carat** is a unit used for measuring the purity of gold: the higher the number of carats, the more pure the gold is.

These pretty rings are available in nine carat gold.

---

carve, carves, carving, carved

calve, calves, calving, calved.

/kɑːv/

---

carve

VERB

The most common uses of **carve** have to do with cutting objects. For example, to **carve** wood means to cut patterns in it or to cut it into a particular shape using sharp tools; to **carve** a large piece of meat means to cut thin slices off it using a knife.

He began to carve his initials on the tree.
Smoked ham is carved in the same way as fresh ham.

● **Carve** also occurs in the following phrasal verbs; **carve out; carve up.**

calve

VERB

When cows **calve**, they give birth.

The cow was not for sale as she was due to calve in October.

Note that **calves** is also the plural form of the noun **calf**. A **calf** is a young cow. Your **calves** are the backs of your legs between your ankles and your knees.

---

cash, cashes, cashing, cashed
cache, caches

/kæʃ/

---

cash

UNCOUNT NOUN

Cash is money, especially in the form of notes and coins rather than cheques.

The cash was being used to pay for food and shelter.
Mr Leah was happier, having finally sold the car for cash.

VERB

To **cash** a cheque means to exchange it for notes and coins.

Crockford's let me cash a cheque, and I advanced him some money.

● **Cash** also occurs in the phrasal verb **cash in**.

cache

COUNT NOUN

A **cache** of things is a quantity of them that have been hidden.

The book is based on a cache of letters from Jeanne to a friend.
...one of the biggest caches of terrorist equipment ever found in Britain.

---

cast, casts, casting, cast
caste, castes

/kɑːst, kæst/

---

cast

Note that the form **cast** is used in the present tense and is also the past tense and past participle form of the verb.

COLLECTIVE COUNT NOUN

The **cast** of a play or film is all the people who act in it.

The audience, like the cast, was young and enthusiastic.

VERB

To **cast** an actor in a particular role means to choose him or her to play that role.

Serena Scott-Thomas landed the role of a lifetime when she was cast as Princess Diana.

VERB

If you **cast** your **eyes** somewhere, you look in that direction.

Graham cast his eyes over the woman beside him.

PHRASE

To **cast doubt on** something means to make people unsure about that thing.

Sadly, recent research has cast doubt on the protective effect of alcohol.

VERB

To **cast** your vote in an election means to vote.

Only about one-third of voters will actually cast their votes tomorrow.

● **Cast** also occurs in the following phrasal verbs: **cast around; cast aside; cast off.**

caste

COUNT NOUN

A **caste** is a social class in Hindu society.

Neither clothes nor profession are a reliable indication of caste.

---

cause, causes, causing, caused

cores

/kɔːz/

---

cause

VERB

To **cause** something to happen means to make it happen.

Typhoons are continuing to cause damage in the region of the South China Sea.
These killings will cause grief to many.

COUNT NOUN

The **cause** of something is the reason why it happens.

Perhaps 2 million Americans have the disease, and it is the fourth leading cause of death among older people.

Nobody knew the cause of the explosion.

cores

COUNT NOUN

Cores is the plural form of the noun 'core'. See **core, corps** for an explanation of the uses of this word.

Prepare fruits by removing any tough stems or cores.

---

ceiling, ceilings
sealing

/sˈiːlɪŋ/

---

ceiling

COUNT NOUN

The **ceiling** of a room is the top inside surface of it.

A boy was sprawled out on the bed staring at the ceiling.

COUNT NOUN

Ceiling can be used to refer to an official upper limit imposed on something. When it is used in this way, it is usually used in the structure '**a ceiling of** a particular amount'.

Last November the thirteen member countries set a production ceiling of 22 million barrels a day.

sealing

Sealing is a noun and the '-ing' form of the verb 'seal'.

VERB

If someone **is sealing** something, they are closing it securely.

Sulphur was burnt before sealing the wine into barrels.
He then repeated the experiment, but instead of sealing the flasks, covered half of them with gauze.

UNCOUNT NOUN

Sealing is the hunting of seals.

...an international dispute with Britain over sealing rights.

---

cereal, cereals
serial, serials

/sˈɪərɪəl/

---

cereal

VARIABLE NOUN

A **cereal** is a plant that produces grain.

The best cereal in dry climates is wheat.

VARIABLE NOUN

Cereal is a breakfast food made of grain.

Some breakfast cereals contain enormous amounts of sugar.

serial

COUNT NOUN

A **serial** is a story which is broadcast or published in a number of parts over a period of time.

TV serials treat violence and law-breaking as normal everyday events.

ADJECTIVE

Serial killings are a number of murders committed by the same person over a period of time.

The novel is about a serial killer in Manhattan.
He has worked on a number of serial murder cases.

---

chased
chaste
/tʃeɪst/

---

chased

Chased is the '-ed' form of the verb 'chase'.

VERB

If one person **chased** another, they ran after the other person in order to try to catch them.

A dozen soldiers chased after the car.

chaste

ADJECTIVE

A **chaste** person does not have sex with anyone, or only has sex with their husband or wife; an old-fashioned word.

Girls are expected to remain chaste until marriage.

---

check, checks, checking, checked
cheque, cheques
/tʃek/

---

check

VERB

To **check** something means to make sure that it is correct.

Check that your ticket is authentic.

A nurse weighs you and checks your blood pressure daily.

COUNT NOUN

A **check** is an inspection to make sure that everything is correct.

A simple check of cash and investments would have revealed the mistake.

VERB

To **check** an undesirable or unpleasant situation means to stop it from continuing or spreading.

The Philippines announced a policy to check fast population growth.

VARIABLE NOUN

Check is a pattern made of squares.

...a tall man in a check suit.
The wallpapers come in tasteful stripes and checks.

COUNT NOUN

In a restaurant in the United States, your **check** is your bill.

He waved to the waiter to get the check.

See also **cheque** below.
● **Check** also occurs in the following phrasal verbs: **check in; check into; check out; check up.**

cheque

COUNT NOUN

A **cheque** is a printed piece of paper that you can use instead of money. Note that in American English this is spelt 'check'.

To order just send a cheque for £24.95.

---

chilli, chillis
chilly, chillier, chilliest

/tʃɪli/

---

chilli

VARIABLE NOUN

A **chilli** is a small red or green vegetable with a hot, spicy taste.

Add chopped pepper and chilli and fry gently for a further 5 minutes.

Note that **chilli** can also be spelt 'chili'.

chilly

ADJECTIVE

Chilly means rather cold and unpleasant.

. . .the chilly waters off the coast of Iceland.

---

choose, chooses, choosing, chose, chosen
chews /tʃuːz/

---

choose

VERB

To **choose** a particular thing means to select it. To **choose** to do a particular thing means to decide to do it when there are other things that you could possibly do.

The party leader can choose the actual day for a vote.
Some women choose to combine homemaking with a career.

chews

Chews is the '-s' form of the verb 'chew'.

VERB

When someone **chews** something, they break it up using their teeth.

He eats so quickly I don't think he always chews his food well.

---

clause, clauses
claws /klɔːz/

---

clause

COUNT NOUN

A **clause** is a section of a legal document.

A clause in his contract pays him roughly 800,000 dollars if he quits before 1990.

COUNT NOUN

In grammar, a **clause** is a group of words which contains a verb. In the sentence 'We won't be getting married until we've saved enough money', 'We won't be getting married' and 'until we've saved enough money' are both clauses.

claws

Claws is the plural form of the noun 'claw'.

COUNT NOUN

Claws are the thin curved nails on an animal's feet.

A cat in ecstasy will extend and retract its claws and purr loudly.

● **Claws** also occurs in the '-s' form of the following phrasal verbs:
claw at; claw back.

---

climb, climbs, climbing, climbed   /klaɪm/
clime, climes

---

climb

VERB

To **climb** something means to move towards the top of it.
Your father is finding it more difficult to climb the stairs.
He quickly climbs the path to the house.

VERB

If things such as prices or amounts **climb**, they increase.
When the price of oil climbs, profits climb as well.
During the day, the temperature climbs and is at its highest in late afternoon.

clime

COUNT NOUN

A particular **clime** is a particular type of climate; a literary word.
The plant flourishes particularly well in slightly harsher climes.

---

colonel, colonels   /kɜːnəl/
kernel, kernels

---

colonel

COUNT NOUN

A **colonel** is an army officer of fairly high rank.
He was soon promoted to colonel.
'Keep cool, men, don't fire yet,' shouted Colonel Corse.

kernel

COUNT NOUN

The **kernel** of a nut is the part inside the shell.
...the kernel of the cocoa bean.

compliment, compliments, complimenting, complimented	/kɒmplɪment/
complement, complements, complementing, complemented	/kɒmplɪmənt/

The verb is pronounced /kɒmplɪment/. The noun is pronounced /kɒmplɪmənt/.

compliment

VERB

To **compliment** someone or something means to praise them.

It always pleases me when guests compliment me on my food.

COUNT NOUN

If you pay someone a **compliment**, you say something nice about them.

You've just paid me the greatest compliment of my life.

complement

VERB

If two things **complement** each other, or if one thing **complements** another, they both have desirable qualities which make a good combination when they are put together.

California wines are available to complement your meal.
This colour complements the others in the paintings.

SINGULAR NOUN

The full **complement** of something is the complete set of it. When **complement** is used in this way, it is usually modified.

In order to perform this work, it was necessary for him to have a full complement of hand tools.

COUNT NOUN

In grammar, a **complement** is a noun group or an adjective which occurs after a verb such as 'be', 'seem', or 'become'. In the sentences 'He is a geologist' and 'Nobody seems amused', 'geologist' and 'amused' are complements.

---

complimentary
complementary
/kɒmplɪmentri/

---

complimentary

ADJECTIVE

If you are **complimentary** about something, you say nice things about it.

Colleagues have been extremely complimentary about my achievements within the department.

ADJECTIVE

Something that is **complimentary** is supplied free of charge.

I expected them to give me a complimentary bottle of champagne.

complementary

ADJECTIVE

If things are **complementary**, they go together well.

Select teams of managers with complementary personalities.

---

conquer, conquers, conquering, conquered
conker, conkers
/kɒŋkəʳ/

---

conquer

VERB

To **conquer** a country means to defeat it in a war.

Around 58 B.C. he launched a campaign to conquer Gaul.

VERB

To **conquer** a difficulty means to overcome it.

If smokers want to conquer their addiction they can be helped to do so.

conker

COUNT NOUN

A **conker** is a nut from the horse chestnut tree; children thread them with string to play **conkers**.

The conker season is here again.
...a game of conkers.

---

core, cores
corps /kɔːʳ/

See also **cause, cores**.

core

COUNT NOUN

The **core** of a fruit is the hard centre of it containing the seeds.

A plate on the chair had an apple core on it.

corps

COUNT NOUN

A **corps** is a part of the army with special duties. Note that **corps** is both the singular and the plural form.

I sent one of the members of the Military Council, to instruct a tank corps in how its resources could best be used.

---

cord, cords
chord, chords /kɔːʳd/

---

cord

VARIABLE NOUN

Cord is a type of strong, thick string.

The door had been tied shut with a length of nylon cord.
Some of the women wore a key on a cord round their necks.

chord

COUNT NOUN

A **chord** is a number of musical notes played together.

I taught myself to play the piano, so I was learning about chords.

---

cornflour
cornflower, cornflowers /kɔːʳnflaʊəʳ/

---

cornflour

UNCOUNT NOUN

Cornflour is very fine white flour made from maize.

In a mixing bowl, beat together the eggs, cornflour and sugar.

cornflower

VARIABLE NOUN

A **cornflower** is a type of small blue flower.

Sow plants such as cornflower and calendula in pots.

---

council, councils
counsel, counsels, counselling, counselled

/ka͟ʊnsəl/

---

council

COUNT NOUN

A **council** is a group of people elected to run a town or other area.

People are eligible to vote for new local and district councils.

COUNT NOUN

A **council** is a group of people who give advice or information about a particular subject. When **council** is used in this way, it is usually modified.

She is a member of the National Council on the Arts.
...the two most important advisory councils that help to decide what is taught in schools.

ADJECTIVE

You rent a **council** house from your local council.

Home was a council house where mum and dad live to this day.

counsel

Note that the '-ing' form and the '-ed' form are spelt 'counseling', 'counseled' in American English.

UNCOUNT NOUN

Counsel is wise advice; a formal use.

Sara was solicitous and offered counel as to how best to deal with it.

VERB

To **counsel** someone to do something means to advise them to do it; a formal use.

It is appropriate, I think, for him to counsel her not to drive.
The prime minister was right to counsel 'severe caution' about military intervention.

VERB

If you **counsel** people, you talk to them about their problems, usually because it is your job to do so.

Dr David Lewis says he has had to counsel couples whose relationships have been ruined by jealousy.

---

councillor, councillors
counsellor, counsellors   /kaʊnsələ^r/

---

councillor

COUNT NOUN

A **councillor** is a member of a local council.

He has served the community in his capacity as a councillor.

counsellor

COUNT NOUN

A **counsellor** is someone whose job is to give advice to people who need it.

Counsellors are trained to give advice and make suggestions.

---

coup, coups
coo, coos, cooing, cooed   /kuː/

---

coup

COUNT NOUN

When there is a **coup**, a group of people sieze power in a country.

That government was overthrown in a military coup three years ago.

coo

VERB

When doves or pigeons **coo**, they make their soft call.

A dove coos above the lush cricket pitch.

VERB

When people **coo**, they make soft loving noises, or they speak in a soft murmur.

She came quickly into the room, greeted Claire, and paused to coo at the baby.

course, courses
coarse, coarser, coarsest

/kɔːᵗs/

course

COUNT NOUN

A **course** is a series of lessons or lectures.

A degree course in War Studies available at London University.

COUNT NOUN

A **course** is a series of medical treatments.

I returned to school after a course of medication.

COUNT NOUN

A particular **course** of a meal is one part of it, served separately from the rest of the meal.

...a first course of pasta.

COUNT NOUN

The **course** taken by a ship or aircraft is the route it takes.

Captain Hadley described a coastguard hearing how the ship's course was changed before the accident.

SINGULAR NOUN

The **course** of events is the way that they develop.

It was one of those ideas that change the course of history.

coarse

ADJECTIVE

Something that is **coarse** is rough in texture.

...a coarse blanket.

ADJECTIVE

If someone is **coarse**, their speech or behaviour is rude.

Foul language and coarse behaviour will not be tolerated.

court, courts
caught

/kɔːt/

court

COUNT NOUN

A **court** is a place where legal matters are decided.

The 28-year-old footballer was in court last week for breaking a rival player's jaw.

COUNT NOUN

A **court** is an area for playing tennis, badminton, or squash.

The hotel is set in four acres of grounds with a swimming pool and tennis court.

COUNT NOUN

The **court** of a king or queen is the place where he or she lives.

...King Arthur's Court.

caught

Caught is the past tense and past participle form of the verb 'catch'.

VERB

The most common uses of **caught** have to do with trapping or taking hold of something that is moving. For example, if an animal **is caught**, it is captured, usually by a trap or other device; if a ball is **caught**, someone takes it out of the air using their hands.

I know of a few people who have caught twenty-pound fish in such lakes.
He caught the ball in mid-air and closed his hand around it.

VERB

If someone has **caught** a disease, they have developed that disease, usually as a result of coming into contact with someone who is already suffering from it.

Doctors who checked them decided they hadn't caught a contagious disease.

VERB

If someone **caught** a bus, train, or aeroplane, they got on it in order to travel to a particular place.

She usually caught the bus outside the hospital.

● **Caught** also occurs in the past tense and past participle forms of the following phrasal verbs: **catch at; catch on; catch out; catch up; catch up on; catch up with.**

coward, cowards
cowered

/ka͟ʊəʳd/

coward

COUNT NOUN

A **coward** is a person who is not brave in dangerous and difficult situations.

He is probably a bit of a coward when having to deal with people face to face.

cowered

Cowered is the '-ed' form of the verb 'cower'.

VERB

If someone **cowered**, they bent downwards or moved back in order to move away or hide from danger.

Tourists and residents cowered behind locked doors in fear and panic.

---

creak, creaks, creaking, creaked
creek, creeks

/kri͟ːk/

creak

VERB

If something **creaks**, it makes a harsh, squeaking sound, for example when it is moved or when weight is put on it.

A branch began to creak in the tree overhead.
The roller coaster creaks and makes a lot of noise.

COUNT NOUN

A **creak** is the harsh squeaking sound something makes when it is moved or when weight is put on it.

He heard the loud creak of the chair as the man rose from it.

creek

COUNT NOUN

A **creek** is a small stream or river.

We did not allow fishing or swimming in the creek.

---

cruise, cruises, cruising, cruised
crews   /kru:z/

---

cruise

COUNT NOUN

A **cruise** is a holiday spent on a ship which visits different places.

They're off to the Mediterranean for a cruise on a luxury yacht.

VERB

When vehicles such as cars, ships, or aeroplanes **cruise**, they move at a constant speed that is comfortable and unhurried.

The company says electric cars will be able to cruise at high speeds.

crews

Crews is the plural form of the noun 'crew'.

COUNT NOUN

The **crews** of ships and aeroplanes are the people who work on them.

The crews of both the boats near us were invited aboard.

---

curb, curbs, curbing, curbed
kerb, kerbs   /kɜːᵇb/

---

curb

VERB

To **curb** something means to control it and keep it within fixed limits.

They were forced either to curb costs or go bankrupt.
The country has no chance of emerging from its economic crisis unless it curbs population growth.

COUNT NOUN

A **curb** on something is a restraint on it.

The report concludes there is a curb on competition in some areas.
Young drivers are facing tough new curbs in a Government bid to cut deaths on the road.

See also **kerb**, on the next page.

kerb

COUNT NOUN

The **kerb** is the part of the pavement next to the road. Note that in American English this is spelt 'curb'.

The twenty-six year old was hit by a passing car when he stepped off the kerb.

---

current, currents
currant, currants
/kʌrənt/

---

current

COUNT NOUN

A **current** is a steady, continuous flowing movement of air or water.
The current of the river is fast flowing and treacherous.

COUNT NOUN

An electric **current** is a flow of electricity.
In radio receivers and television sets, the signals are very feeble electric currents.

ADJECTIVE

Something that is **current** is happening now.
The collapse of the US currency undoubtedly triggered the current crisis.

currant

COUNT NOUN

A **currant** is a small dried grape.
In a bowl, stir the currants into the grated carrots.

---

damn, damns, damning, damned
dam, dams, damming, dammed
/dæm/

---

damn

'Damn' is a mild swear word.
Damn! I'm out of cigarettes!

VERB

To **damn** something means to criticise or complain about it in a way that makes it seem worthless or wicked.

51

I interpreted every bit of evidence as damning her further.
I don't see why I should be damned for something I did not do.

dam

COUNT NOUN

A **dam** is a wall built across a river to stop the flow of water and make a lake.

The plan was to build several dams across the Irtysh.

VERB

To **dam** a river means to build a dam across it.

Plans to dam the nearby Delaware River began after a flood in 1955.
The stream could be dammed to form a pond.

---

days
daze
/deɪz/

---

days

Days is the plural form of the noun 'day'.

VARIABLE NOUN

Days are the seven twenty-four hour periods of time in a week.

Just a few days ago she came to my house to discuss her latest project.

VARIABLE NOUN

Days are the periods of time between dawn and dusk when it is light.

The fire raged for three days and nights.

daze

PHRASE

If you are **in a daze**, you are confused and unable to think clearly.

She walked back to her tent in a daze.

---

dear, dearer, dearest
deer
/dɪəʳ/

---

dear

VOCATIVE

You can call someone **dear** to show affection.

I'm sure they will take good care of you, dear.

ADJECTIVE

If something is **dear** to you, you care about it very much.

...a region that was dear to him.

CONVENTION

You write **'Dear'** before someone's name at the beginning of a letter

Dear Brian, I'm writing this so I can be the first to tell you.

PHRASE

You say **'oh dear'** when you are sad or upset about something.

Oh dear, I'm afraid I'm getting confused.

ADJECTIVE

Something that is **dear** costs a lot of money.

The ammunition is very dear for them to buy.

deer

COUNT NOUN

A **deer** is a large animal with antlers. Note that **deer** is both the singular and the plural form.

If he gets hungry, he'll kill a deer.

---

desert, deserts, deserting, deserted
dessert, desserts   /dɪzɜːʳt/

---

desert

VERB

To **desert** a place means to leave it. To **desert** a person means to leave them and to refuse to help or support them.

She wasn't going to desert her son.
She is married to an American naval officer who callously deserts her.

Note that **desert** can also be pronounced /dezəʳt/, and that it has a different meaning when it is pronounced in this way; a desert is a dry, rocky place.

dessert

VARIABLE NOUN

Dessert is the sweet course at the end of a meal.

die, dye

They were finishing off their dinner with coffee and dessert.

---

die, dies, dying, died
dye, dyes, dyeing, dyed   /d<u>aɪ</u>/

---

die

VERB

To **die** means to stop living.

I hope my mum is not going to die.
Most of her potted plants had died from neglect.

dye

MASS NOUN

A **dye** is a substance used to colour things.

Natural dyes have a tendency to fade in washing or light.

VERB

To **dye** something means to change the colour of it with a dye.

It is a good idea to dye the fabric to match the main colour of the rug.

---

disc, discs
disk, disks   /d<u>ɪ</u>sk/

---

disc

COUNT NOUN

A **disc** is a flat circular object.

Hilton's face was gray, his eyes like flat discs of metal.

COUNT NOUN

A **disc** is one of the parts of your spine.

He underwent surgery last year to correct a disc problem.

disk

COUNT NOUN

A **disk** is a flat circular metal plate used by a computer to store information.

Inside the safe had been five computer disks.

---

discreet
discrete

/dɪskri:t/

---

discreet

ADJECTIVE

If you are **discreet**, you are polite and careful in what you say or do, because you want to avoid embarrassing or offending someone.

They were gossipy and not always discreet.
He followed at a discreet distance.

ADJECTIVE

If you are **discreet** about something you are doing, you do not tell other people about it, in order to avoid being embarrassed or to gain an advantage.

We were very discreet about the romance.
She's making a few discreet enquiries with her mother's friends.

ADJECTIVE

Something that is **discreet** does not draw much attention to itself.

It was a discreet flat in a quiet street.

discrete

ADJECTIVE

Discrete things are separate from each other; a formal word.

These blocks should be considered as discrete units.

---

dough, doughs
doe, does

/doʊ/

---

dough

VARIABLE NOUN

Dough is a mixture of flour and water which can be cooked to make bread or biscuits.

Spread the softened butter over the surface of the dough.
These doughs can be mixed and rolled out immediately.

doe

COUNT NOUN

A **doe** is an adult female deer, rabbit, or hare.

A doe crossed the clearing and grazed briefly.

Note that **does** can also be pronounced /dəz/, and that when it is pronounced in this way it is the '-s' form of the verb 'do'.

---

draft, drafts, drafting, drafted
draught, draughts

/drɑːft, dræft/

---

draft

COUNT NOUN

A **draft** of something such as a letter, book, or speech is an early version of it.

Parliament today will discuss the first draft of a new election bill.

VERB

To **draft** something such as a letter, book, or speech means to create the first version of it.

The parties to the talks are said to be trying to draft a letter of intent.

VERB

To **draft** people into the armed forces means to tell them that they have to serve in them or they will face criminal charges.

If a war comes, they're going to draft people.

VERB

To **draft** people to a place means to send them to that place in order to do a particular job.

The murders leave the local police chief baffled, so he drafts in help from the next county.

draught

COUNT NOUN

A **draught** is a current of air.

Exposed floorboards should be sealed to cut down on draughts.

COUNT NOUN

If someone takes a **draught** of a drink, they swallow a large amount of it.

Kelly took a long draught from his beer.

PLURAL NOUN

Draughts is a game for two people, played with round pieces on a chequered board.

He'd like to show the boy how to play draughts.

draw, draws, drawing, drew
drawer, drawers

/drɔː/

draw

VERB

To **draw** means to make pictures with a pencil or pen.

...a boy who liked to draw.
He also draws a cartoon strip for The Beano.

VERB

When people **draw** away or **draw** near, they move away or move near.

As we draw near the loudspeakers are producing a thick wall of sound.
She tried to catch Marcia's eye, to draw her from the table.

VERB

To **draw** a vehicle means to pull it.

Black horses used to draw the hearses.

VERB

To **draw** curtains means to open or close them.

Draw the curtains if you are going out for the evening.

VERB

If the two teams involved in a game **draw**, both teams have the same score at the end of the game.

What will happen if Zaire draws with Brazil?

COUNT NOUN

A **draw** is a game that ends with both teams having the same score.

The second Test against Australia ended in a draw in Colombo yesterday.

● **Draw** also occurs in the following phrasal verbs: **draw into;
draw on; draw up; draw upon.**

drawer

COUNT NOUN

A **drawer** is a box shaped part of a desk or other piece of furniture which slides open.

The top drawer of his desk slid open easily.

dual
duel, duels /djuːəl/

dual

ADJECTIVE

Dual means having two parts, functions, or aspects.

In 1970, only 39 per cent of all households reported dual incomes.

duel

COUNT NOUN

A **duel** is a fight between two people using swords or pistols.

He would on principle have refused to fight a duel.

COUNT NOUN

A **duel** is a conflict between two people.

Two runners were evenly matched, mentally and physically, in the duel for the gold medal.

---

due
dew /djuː/

due

PREPOSITION

If one thing is **due to** another, it happens because of the other thing.

That this work had not been done was not due to a lack of ability and talent.

ADJECTIVE

If something is **due** at a particular time, it is expected to happen or arrive at that time.

The fire brigades' pay award is due at the beginning of next month. What time is the bus due?

ADJECTIVE

If some money is **due to** you, you have a right to it.

Debt due to former shareholders was substantially reduced.

ADJECTIVE

If you give something **due** consideration, you give it the consideration it deserves.

After due consideration of the evidence, the meeting decided that no one had been to blame.

Everyone has to exercise due care and attention for the environment.

dew

UNCOUNT NOUN

Dew is small drops of water which form on the ground in the night.

The grass was wet with dew, too wet to sit on.

---

earn, earns, earning, earned

urn, urns

/$\mathbf{\underline{3}}$:^{r}n/

---

earn

VERB

To **earn** money means to receive money for work that you do.

I earn 264 roubles a month.

...the 15 dollars an hour an experienced timber worker earns.

VERB

If something **earns** money, it produces money as profit.

The bond has to be held for 12 months before it earns any interest at all.

VERB

If you **earn** something such as praise or success, you get it because you deserve it.

The effects of what happened at Chernobyl will earn a place in the history books.

urn

COUNT NOUN

An **urn** is a type of vase or jar.

...stone urns filled to overflowing with trailing ivy.

COUNT NOUN

An **urn** is a large container used for making large quantities of hot drinks such as tea or coffee.

Laurie was pouring boiling water into the top of a big coffee urn.

faint, faints, fainting, fainted; fainter, faintest
feint, feints
/f**ei**nt/

faint

ADJECTIVE

Something that is **faint** is not very strong or intense.

The images on the video will be large and faint.
It was only by luck that a man walking his dog heard Matthew
Davies' faint cries for help.

VERB

To **faint** means to lose consciousness for a short time.

If someone faints, keep him lying down and loosen his clothes at the
neck, chest, and waist.

feint

COUNT NOUN

In a fight or battle, a **feint** is a misleading action or movement
which is intended to deceive your oppponent.

The danger is that the North will make a feint in the direction of peace
simply to play for time.

fair, fairs, fairer, fairest
fare, fares, faring, fared
/f**eə**r/

fair

ADJECTIVE

Something that is **fair** is reasonable, right, or just.

He declined to comment on the leaked report, but said that his
colleague's remarks 'seemed fair'.
The two leading opposition parties have repeatedly said they do not
believe fair elections are possible.

ADJECTIVE

A **fair** amount of something is quite a large amount of it.

You have to have guts, real knowledge and a fair bit of money.

ADJECTIVE

Someone who has **fair** hair has light, blonde hair. Someone who has
fair skin has very pale skin.

She has blue eyes and fair hair.
There is now a much wider choice of these fabulous fake tans to suit different skin colours, even the very fair.

COUNT NOUN

A **fair** is an event to display, sell, or advertise things. When **fair** is used in this way, it is usually modified.

...the East Berkshire Antiques Fair.
About 3,000 exhibitors were at the fair this year.

COUNT NOUN

A **fair** is an event held in a park or field which people go to to enjoy themselves by playing games or riding on various machines.

My mum used to take me to the fair there.

fare

COUNT NOUN

The **fare** is the money you have to pay for a journey on public transport.

The return fare from London to Nice by train is £152.80.

VERB

If you **fare** well in a particular situation, you do well. If you **fare** badly, you do badly.

They seem to fare less well in the task of anticipating new forms of attack.
An international analysis of executives' salaries concludes that British managers fare better than most of their counterparts abroad.

UNCOUNT NOUN

You can refer to a particular type of food as a particular **fare**.

The menu is simple—nothing fancy, just solid German fare.

---

fate, fates
fête, fêtes   /feɪt/

---

fate

COUNT NOUN

Someone's **fate** is what happens to them. When **fate** is used in this way, it is usually modified.

There's some confusion over the fate of the five hundred or so passengers.

The fates of other countries should matter to us.

UNCOUNT NOUN

Fate is a power believed by some people to control everything that happens.

Fate has been unkind to them.

fête

COUNT NOUN

A **fête** is an outdoor event that includes competitions, entertainments, and the sale of home-made goods.

The warm weather has meant that fêtes, festivals, parties and weddings have been terrific successes.

---

father, fathers, fathering, fathered
farther

/fɑːðəʳ/

---

father

COUNT NOUN

Your **father** is your male parent.

His father Keith was a distinguished national hunt jockey.

TITLE

In some Christian churches, priests are addressed or referred to as 'Father'.

Father Subev believes his Church will have to make changes if it is to regain its credibility.

VERB

To **father** a child means to make a woman pregnant so that a child is born; a literary use.

There are hundreds of thousands of men around the world who are unable to father a child.

farther

ADJECTIVE

Farther is the comparative form of the adjective 'far'. 'Far' is a frequently used adjective. You are probably familiar with the uses shown in the examples below. Look in a COBUILD dictionary if you need a fuller explanation of the uses of this word.

All cars coming along the only other road are stopped by police and prevented from going farther.

The Suruga site is farther away but the earthquake there could be more powerful.
Farther north, in the Jaffna peninsula, government aircraft have been bombing civilian areas.
The Chancellor indicated that inflation could rise still farther.
...a cabinet farther to the right than any that have gone before.

---

feet

feat, feats

/fiːt/

---

feet

Feet is the plural form of the noun 'foot'.

COUNT NOUN

Your **feet** are the parts of your body at the end of your legs that you walk on.

Both men had bruises on their hands and feet.
There was ice under my feet and I slipped and fell.

COUNT NOUN

Feet are units of length.

We soon passed through the layer of cloud and were cruising above it at 13,000 feet.
There are also foam rubber wedges we've suspended here on the metal grid several feet above the real floor.

feat

COUNT NOUN

A **feat** is an impressive and difficult act.

Three factors helped Japanese companies pull off this feat.
...a truly remarkable feat.

---

find, finds, finding, found

fined

/faɪnd/

---

find

VERB

The most common uses of **find** have to do with discovering or seeing someone or something, or with learning where they are. For example, if you **find** an object that you have lost, you discover where it is; if you **find** a place to stay, you learn of a house or hotel where you can stay.

> *...if you wanted to find underground water in a desert.*
> *...various efforts to find a peaceful solution.*
> *Young people without families may find Brussels boring.*
> *He awoke to find a fireman in his smoke filled room.*
> *I find cooking relaxing.*

● **Find** also occurs in the phrasal verb **find out**.

fined

Fined is the '-ed' form of the verb 'fine'.

VERB

If someone **is fined** a particular sum of money, they are made to pay that sum of money as punishment for something that they have done.

The club was fined 150 million lire.
US West has been fined 10 million dollars for discriminatory pricing.

---

flair

flare, flares, flaring, flared   /fle͟ə^r/

---

flair

SINGULAR NOUN OR UNCOUNT NOUN

If you have a **flair** for something, you have a natural ability to do it.

He had a great flair for getting on with people.
She has lost none of her flair for chilling stories.

UNCOUNT NOUN

If you do something with **flair**, you do it in a stylish and original way.

Henderson Forsythe played the old father with comic flair.

flare

COUNT NOUN

A **flare** is a device producing a bright flame which is used as a signal.

...a military flare from a crashed aircraft.

VERB

If bad situations **flare**, they suddenly arise or become much worse.

In Washington, meanwhile, arguments flare between those urging the President to take action, and those who would prefer him not to get involved.

● **Flare** also occurs in the phrasal verb **flare up**.

---

flawed
floored

/flɔːd/

---

flawed

ADJECTIVE

If something is **flawed**, it has a fault of some kind and is therefore not as good as it should be.

...claims that the design of the ship was flawed.
The special prize went to a flawed but remarkable first film by 33-year-old Mario Martone.

floored

VERB

Floored is the '-ed' form of the verb 'floor'. See **floor, flaw** for an explanation of the uses of this word.

McAuley was floored twice in the second round and again at the start of the third.
In the late 1970s he was almost floored by a series of flops.

---

flee, flees, fleeing, fled
flea, fleas

/fliː/

---

flee

VERB

If you **flee**, you run away from a place, person, or thing.

Conditions in the country are forcing people to flee.
...a young girl who falls to her death as she flees her pursuer.

flea

COUNT NOUN

A **flea** is a type of insect.

...a very small water flea which lives in the pond.

flew
flu   /fl**u:**/
flue, flues

flew

Flew is the past tense form of the verb 'fly'.

VERB

If something **flew**, it moved through the air.

The bird flew away.
Our journey began by military helicopter which flew at an altitude of less than two hundred feet.

VERB

If someone **flew** somewhere, they travelled there in an aircraft.

She flew back to New York.
He flew by helicopter from the US naval air base.

flu

UNCOUNT NOUN

Flu is an illness which is like a bad cold.

His parents thought he had flu.

flue

COUNT NOUN

A **flue** is a chimney or a pipe that acts like a chimney.

He filled the fireplace with so much wood that the flue was blocked.

---

floor, floors, flooring, floored
flaw, flaws   /fl**ɔ:**/

See also **flawed, floored**.

floor

COUNT NOUN

The **floor** of a room is the part you walk on.

There were clothes strewn over the floor.
The jar fell on the floor and broke.

COUNT NOUN

A particular **floor** of a building is a particular level of it.

...an office on the second floor.
There was often only one toilet per floor.

VERB

To **floor** someone means to make them fall on the ground, usually by knocking or hitting them.

Chitalada unleashed eight successive punches to floor his opponent.

VERB

If events or questions **floor** you, you are so surprised or confused by them that you cannot react to them properly.

She gave him a smile that was intended to floor him.
Sometimes Juliana floors the listener with a sly, unexpected observation.

flaw

COUNT NOUN

A **flaw** is a fault or a mistake.

Critics claim that it is a serious flaw.
He had repeatedly warned of flaws in the operation.

---

flow, flows, flowing, flowed
floe, floes

/fl<u>ou</u>/

---

flow

VERB

If something such as a liquid or a large group of people **flows** from one place to another, it moves steadily and continuously from one place to another.

As soon as you turn the switch, electric current begins to flow through the wires in the lamp.
Refugees flow from one country to another.

COUNT NOUN

A **flow** of something is a steady, continuous movement of it from one place to another.

Leonardo avidly studied the flow of water in pipes.
A stroke is a sudden disruption in the flow of blood to an area of the brain.

VERB

If things such as hair or material **flow**, they hang freely or loosely.

He folds his hands and lets his long black hair flow over his shoulders.
The fabric must be such that it flows with the body.

floe

COUNT NOUN

An ice **floe** is a large area of ice floating in the sea.

The end of the last Ice Age saw a rise in sea levels as ice floes melted.

---

flower, flowers, flowering, flowered
flour, flours

/flaʊəʳ/

flower

COUNT NOUN

A **flower** is the coloured or white part of a plant which grows on a stem.

Each flower is composed of three petals.
...the New York wholesale flower market.

COUNT NOUN

A **flower** is a small plant which has flowers.

She took to planting flowers and vegetables in vacant lots.

VERB

When plants **flower**, they produce flowers.

Modern roses are bred to flower more or less continuously throughout the summer season.

VERB

If plans or ideas **flower**, they develop fully and have good results.

He has brief enthusiasms, but they are destroyed before they can flower.

flour

MASS NOUN

Flour is a white or brown powder that is made by grinding grain.

I have had consistently good results using bread flour for pasta doughs.
Combine the flour with 3 tablespoons of water.
Most bakers use the same blend of ordinary flours as the base for all their loaves.

for
four
fore

/fɔːʳ/

for

Note that **for** can also be pronounced /fəʳ/. It is pronounced /fɔːʳ/ at the end of a sentence of when you want to emphasize it (this is known as the strong form), and /fəʳ/ in all other cases (this is known as the weak form).

PREPOSITION

For is a frequently used preposition. You are probably familiar with the uses shown in the examples below. Look in a COBUILD dictionary if you need a fuller explanation of the uses of this word.

...the elaborate library he'd built especially for her.
She appears nightly on the television news speaking for the State Department.
Life is going to be a lot easier for him without her around.
I was really ashamed of her. But I'm so sorry for her too.
We live in a small house and haven't much room for large laundry machines.
The correspondence went on for a long time.
If you find yourself in China, you can run for miles along the Great Wall.

four

NUMBER

Four is the number 4.

The chorus appears in four out of the seven scenes.
The Secretary of State has had more than four hours of talks with his Soviet counterpart.

fore

PHRASE

If someone or something comes **to the fore**, they suddenly become important or popular.

Rivalries within the opposition may now come to the fore.

fought
fort, forts

/f<u>ɔ</u>ːt/

fought

Fought is the past tense and past participle of 'fight'.

VERB

If someone **fought** something, they tried in a determined way to stop it.

Some of the parents fought the court decision for the removal of their children.
The public fought the uncontrolled spread of fraudulent patent medicines.

VERB

If someone **fought** to achieve something, they worked hard to achieve it.

Women have fought to get and keep union recognition.
I told him how we had fought to hold on to the company.

VERB

If two or more people **fought**, they tried to hurt each other physically.

Many female rebels fought the advancing troops hand to hand.

VERB

If two or more people **fought**, they quarrelled.

The doctor told me I had to start exercising. I argued, I fought, but he was adamant.

● **Fought** also occurs in the past tense forms of the following phrasal verbs: **fight back; fight off; fight out.**

fort

COUNT NOUN

A **fort** is a strong building used by an army for defence.
For their part, the garrison remained determined to defend the fort.

---

foul, fouls, fouling, fouled; fouler, foulest   /faʊl/
fowl, fowls

---

foul

ADJECTIVE

Something that is **foul** is dirty or smelly.

The foul air is generated by the heavy traffic.
The water in the pools became tepid and foul.

ADJECTIVE

Foul language is rude and offensive.

Hurley winced at the memory of the conversation, and the foul
language the man had used.

ADJECTIVE

If someone is in a **foul** mood, or if they are **foul**, they are very
unpleasant.

Your husband is in a really foul temper.

VERB

To **foul** something means to make it dirty.

The largest oil slick in history continues to foul the beaches of Kuwait
and Saudi Arabia.

COUNT NOUN

In sport, a **foul** is an action that is against the rules.

The goal was disallowed because of a foul on the goalkeeper.

● **Foul** also occurs in the phrasal verb **foul up**.

fowl

COUNT NOUN

A **fowl** is a bird, especially one that can be eaten as food. Note that
the plural form can be **fowl** or **fowls**.

Outside, half a dozen thin fowls scratched hopefully for maggots.

---

fourth   /fɔːʳθ/
forth

---

fourth

ADJECTIVE

The **fourth** item in a series is the one that you count as number 4.

71

freeze, frees, frieze

This is the fourth bomb explosion in the capital in recent weeks.

forth

ADVERB

If someone goes **forth** from a place, they leave it; a literary use.

He told Maria that she must go forth and carry on the struggle.

---

freeze, freezes, freezing, froze
frees   /friːz/
frieze, friezes

---

freeze

VERB

When substances **freeze**, they are so cold that they become solid and hard.

The River Thames would freeze solid in those days.
Salty water doesn't freeze as easily as fresh water.
The cold is so terrific that even the oil freezes in motorized vehicles.

VERB

To **freeze** food means to preserve it by keeping it at a temperature below freezing point.

Pack and freeze the cooked potato scones for up to one month.
One of the fish that freezes best is cod.

VERB

To **freeze** means to become so cold so that temperatures are below freezing point.

Cold weather continues to freeze much of the US.

VERB

To **freeze** means to be motionless.

Okay, everybody freeze!

VERB

To **freeze** an amount means to fix it at a certain level.

Continental Airlines says it will freeze wages for six months for all non-management employees.

● **Freeze** also occurs in the following phrasal verbs: **freeze over**; **freeze up**.

frees

Frees is the '-s' form of the verb 'free'.

VERB

If an organization **frees** someone it has been holding prisoner, it releases them.

The group has extended its deadline for the state government to release all its members and sympathisers before it frees two hostages.

VERB

If an event or a situation **frees** something, it makes it available for a particular purpose.

This frees up millions of dollars in bank capital.

frieze

COUNT NOUN

A **frieze** is a decoration along a wall.

It had a few statues and a wonderful frieze painted in green and gold around the walls.

---

fur, furs
fir, firs

/fɜːʳ/

---

fur

UNCOUNT NOUN

Fur is the thick hair on an animal's body.

The creature's fur is short, dense, and silky.

MASS NOUN

You use **fur** to refer to the fur-covered skin of an animal used to make clothes or rugs.

...a beautiful fur coat.
Official reports say some furs are brought by smugglers.

fir

COUNT NOUN

A **fir** is a type of tree.

...thick woods of oaks and firs.

---

gamble, gambles, gambling, gambled
gambol, gambols, gambolling, gambolled   /gæmbªl/

---

gamble

COUNT NOUN

A **gamble** is a risky action.

It's a gamble, but I am willing to do it.
He has built an empire through a series of gambles that often succeeded.

VERB

To **gamble** means to take a risky action.

Investors were willing to gamble on new technologies.
He realized he was gambling with his life.

VERB

To **gamble** means to bet money in a game or on the result of a competition.

She decided to gamble her £300 prize money.
Men and women were gambling more money than they could afford.

gambol

VERB

If animals or people **gambol**, they jump around in a playful way.

A dog came gambolling down the avenue to meet me.

---

gate, gates
gait   /geɪt/

---

gate

COUNT NOUN

A **gate** is a structure like a door which is used at the entrance to a field, a garden, or the grounds of a building

After a hundred yards or so I reached the gate to a field.
The gate was padlocked.

gait

SINGULAR NOUN

Someone's **gait** is their way of walking; a literary word. When **gait** is used in this way, it is always modified.

...a fragile-looking, fleshless figure with the gait of an old man.

geyser, geysers
geezer, geezers

/gi:zə^r/

geyser

COUNT NOUN

A **geyser** is a spring that spouts hot water.

The 2.2 million acres of the park, in Wyoming, Montana and Idaho, contain 60 per cent of the world's geysers.

geezer

COUNT NOUN

Some people use **geezer** to refer to a man; an informal word.

'I don't know this geezer,' he told Mclaren.

great, greater, greatest
grate, grates, grating, grated

/greɪt/

See also **greater, grater**.

great

ADJECTIVE

You use **great** to describe something that is very large in size, degree, or amount.

A great many people were killed.
We have spent a great deal of time understanding the society we live in.

ADJECTIVE

Something or someone that is important, famous, or exciting can be described as **great**.

The great themes of love and death dominate.
...reproductions of paintings and sculptures by great artists.

ADJECTIVE

If something is **great**, it is very good; an informal use.

They had a really great time.

grate

COUNT NOUN

A **grate** is the metal bars in a fireplace.

Beauchamp knelt down and threw a pine log onto the grate.

75

VERB

To **grate** food means to shred it into small pieces with a grater.

Grate the onion and carrots directly into the bowl.

VERB

If objects **grate**, they make a harsh noise because they are being dragged or scraped against something else.

Leaphorn jolted the crate over a boulder faster than he should have and heard the bottom grate against stone.

VERB

If things **grate**, or if they **grate on** you, they irritate you.

The coyness of the candidates is beginning to grate.
As the years went by his nastiness began to grate on his readers.

---

greater
grater, graters

/ɡreɪtəʳ/

---

greater

ADJECTIVE

Greater is the comparative form of the adjective 'great'. See **great, grate** for an explanation of the uses of this word.

She soon realized she needed a greater knowledge of accounting and finance.
Women's increased representation on the workforce has led to to a greater degree of financial independence.
Descartes was an even greater mathematician than philosopher.

ADJECTIVE

Greater is used with or as part of the names of large cities when you are referring to the whole city and the suburbs, rather than just the central part.

...Greater Manchester police.
...the eight million people in greater Calcutta.

grater

COUNT NOUN

A **grater** is a metal tool for shredding food.

Use the finest part of an ordinary grater for grating fresh ginger.

grill, grills, grilling, grilled
grille, grilles

/grɪl/

grill

VERB

To **grill** food means to cook it using strong heat directly above or below it.

Do you have to grill both sides of a beefburger?
Grill for about 2 to 3 minutes on each side.

COUNT NOUN

A **grill** is a part of a cooker where food is cooked by strong heat from above.

By now the kidneys were sizzling on the grill.

VERB

If you **grill** someone, you ask them a lot of questions in an intense way; an informal use.

She is a tough negotiator who grills her clients minutely.

grille

COUNT NOUN

A **grille** is a protective metal grid.

Its ground-floor windows were protected by heavy grilles.

grisly, grislier, grisliest
grizzly

/grɪzli/

grisly

ADJECTIVE

Something that is **grisly** is nasty and horrific.

It was essentially just a grisly and sensational murder story.
The conference heard grisly stories of murder and torture .

grizzly

COUNT NOUN

A **grizzly** or a **grizzly bear** is a large, fierce bear which lives in western North America.

One goat was found dead, killed by a grizzly bear.

grown

groan, groans, groaning, groaned

/gr<u>ou</u>n/

grown

Grown is an adjective and the past participle form of the verb 'grow'.

VERB

A person or thing that **has grown** has increased in size.

The business has grown rapidly because it can generate huge profits.
She'd grown four or five inches in the last year.

VERB

When plants **are grown**, they are planted in the ground and looked after so that they get bigger.

The same foods grown on different soils of the world vary greatly.
...plants grown from seed.

ADJECTIVE

A **grown** man or woman is an adult.

I have two grown daughters and a teenage son.

● **Grown** also occurs in the past participle forms of the following phrasal verbs: **grow apart; grow into; grow on; grow out of; grow up.**

groan

VERB

To **groan** means to make a moaning noise.

I was too sick to move, or to do anything except groan.
He heard Mrs Stakowski groan and say she was sorry.

guerrilla, guerrillas
gorilla, gorillas

/gər<u>i</u>lə/

guerrilla

COUNT NOUN

A **guerrilla** is a person who fights in an unofficial army, usually against the official army.

Declared to be spies or guerrillas, they were shot or hanged soon after capture.

gorilla

COUNT NOUN

A **gorilla** is an animal which resembles a very large ape.

A big bush fire is threatening the home of the famous African mountain gorillas.

---

guest, guests
guessed

/gest/

guest

COUNT NOUN

A **guest** is someone who is staying in your home, or is attending an event because they have been invited.

Mrs. Howard urged a slice of coffee cake upon her guest.
Mr Kinnock was a guest at a dinner in honour of the President.

guessed

Guessed is the '-ed' form of the verb 'guess'.

VERB

If you **guessed** something, you gave an answer or an opinion about something when you did not know whether it was correct.

She was in her late thirties, Brian guessed.
She was Hispanic, probably Puerto Rican, Fleck guessed.

VERB

You can say that you **guessed** something when you gave the correct answer to a question or problem, although you did not know the answer for certain.

She'd guessed right—that Ted Isaacs wasn't eager to have her move in.
I suspect she's guessed that I'm thrilled at the idea.

---

guild, guilds
gild, gilds, gilding, gilded

/gɪld/

---

guild

COUNT NOUN

A **guild** is an organization of people who do the same job or share a particular interest. When **guild** is used in this way, it is usually modified.

guilt, gilt

...the Screen Actors' Guild.
...the Townswomen's Guild.

gild

VERB

To **gild** something means to cover it with gold paint, or to make it look as if it has been covered with gold paint.

Over seven tons of gold were used to gild the interior of the church.

---

guilt
gilt

/gɪlt/

---

guilt

UNCOUNT NOUN

Guilt is an unhappy feeling that you have done something wrong, or that something is your fault.

Had she been nursing feelings of guilt, of remorse, of terrible regret?
She felt a nasty little twinge of guilt.

UNCOUNT NOUN

Guilt is the fact that you have done something wrong or illegal.

You must have no doubt at all about the guilt of the defendant.

gilt

UNCOUNT NOUN

Gilt is a thin layer of gold or gold paint that you use to decorate something.

...pictures in elaborate gilt frames.

---

hail, hails, hailing, hailed
hale

/heɪl/

---

hail

SINGULAR NOUN

Hail consists of tiny balls of ice which fall from the sky like rain.

The hail didn't come as predicted.

VERB

To **hail** means to rain hail.

It started to hail—huge great stones bouncing off the back of my coat.

VERB

To **hail** someone means to call them; a literary use.

We hail her from the doorway.
Outside the bar he had tried to hail a cab.

VERB

If you **hail** a person, event, or achievement **as** important or successful, you praise them publicly.

The National Party was quick to hail the result as a convincing victory.

hale

ADJECTIVE

Someone who is **hale** is healthy; a literary word.

He's tremendously hale and fit-looking.

---

hair, hairs
hare, hares

/he̱ə^r/

---

hair

COUNT NOUN

A **hair** is a long fine strand that grows from your skin.

He didn't leave one shred of evidence in the back seat, not a fibre, a hair, a fingerprint.
You have great big hairs in your ears, why don't you cut them?

UNCOUNT NOUN

Your **hair** is the large number of hairs that grow in a mass on your head.

Even when you were born, you had a head full of thick brown hair.
He had very long hair.

hare

COUNT NOUN

A **hare** is an animal like a large rabbit.

A hare appeared on the opposite verge, quivered for a second, then ran swiftly up the road.

hall, halls
haul, hauls, hauling, hauled

/hɔːl/

hall

COUNT NOUN

A **hall** is the area just inside the front door of a house.

I followed her to the front hall and helped her on with her coat.
Yellow is a good colour for halls and alcoves.

COUNT NOUN

A **hall** is a large room used for events such as meetings or concerts.

She is guaranteed to get a rapturous reception today when she enters the main hall at the Tory conference.
...an orchestral concert in the Albert Hall in London.

haul

VERB

To **haul** something heavy somewhere means to pull it there with great effort.

It took 90 minutes to haul one cow to safety using slings and a winch.

hangar, hangars
hanger, hangers

/hæŋəʳ/

hangar

COUNT NOUN

A **hangar** is a building where aircraft are kept.

The huge transport plane taxied over potholes toward an enormous hangar.

hanger

COUNT NOUN

A **hanger** is a curved piece of metal or wood for hanging clothes on.

Tamsin was struggling to get Gloria's discarded dress back on its hanger.

---

heal, heals, healing, healed
heel, heels /hiːl/

---

heal

VERB

When wounds **heal**, they become healthy again.

What can I do to help my leg ulcer to heal?
This will actually slow the rate at which the wound heals.

VERB

To **heal** an illness means to cure it.

The woman was taught how to heal virtually every illness with the plants.

● **Heal** also occurs in the phrasal verb **heal up**.

heel

COUNT NOUN

Your **heel** is the back part of your foot, just below the ankle.
She gave a little push with her heel.

---

heard
herd, herds, herding, herded /hɜːʳd/

heard

VERB

Heard is the past tense and past participle of the verb 'hear'. See **here, hear** for an explanation of the uses of this word.

He thought he heard footsteps on the marble stairs.
The judge who heard the case was a friend of the sheriff.
He left here early this morning, and I haven't heard from him since.
I can see every word I've heard about you is true.

herd

COUNT NOUN

A **herd** of animals such as cows or deer is a group of them.
I looked out the window and saw a herd of cattle in a pasture.

VERB

To **herd** animals such as cows or deer means to make them move together to form a group.
Stefano had been using a motorcycle to herd the sheep.

here
hear, hears, hearing, heard

/hɪə^r/

See also **here's, hears**; **heard, herd**.

here

Here is a frequently used adverb. You are probably familiar with the uses shown in the examples below. Look in a COBUILD dictionary if you need a fuller explanation of the uses of this word.

Is that why you brought him here for dinner?
You have to sign here and acknowledge the receipt.
The autumn's really here at last.
Here she is.
O'Neill, decisively influenced by the Greeks, is trying here to write pure tragedy.
Here you are—my address.

hear

If you **hear** a sound, you become aware of it through your ears.

You'll hear everything from reggae to waltzes.
Etta hated to hear Mrs Hochstadt talk like that.
She could hear clearly.

To **hear** something such as a complaint means to officially consider it.

The Supreme Court then announced that it would hear the case.

To **hear from** someone means to receive a letter or telephone call from them.

Hope to hear from you soon.
The police say they're anxious to hear from anyone who may know the whereabouts of the firearms.

If you **hear** some news or information, you learn of it because someone tells you, or because it is on the radio or television.

I hear you left your job.

here's
hears

/hɪəʳz/

here's

Here's is the usual spoken form of 'here is'.

Here's our southern Africa correspondent, Mike Wooldridge.
Here's how it's done.

hears

VERB

Hears is the '-s' form of the verb 'hear'. See **here, hear** for an explanation of the uses of this word.

She doesn't begin to read again until she hears her mother on the stairs.
The court is so backlogged, it could be months until it hears the case.
Your doctor will be pleased when he hears that you are visiting India.
He'll do that until he hears that we've suddenly changed direction.

---

heroin
heroine, heroines

/herəʊɪn/

heroin

UNCOUNT NOUN

Heroin is a powerful addictive drug.

He died of an overdose of heroin.

heroine

COUNT NOUN

The **heroine** of a book, film, or play is its main female character.

He published a short novel in 1881 whose heroine was a woman artist.

COUNT NOUN

If you describe a woman as your **heroine**, you mean that you admire her greatly.

This unnamed princess became a heroine to the feminists of China and Japan.

hey
hay
/heɪ/

hey

CONVENTION

You say or shout **'hey!'** to gain someone's attention, or to express surprise or amazement.

Behind him he heard a voice shouting 'Hey You! Get out of there.'

hay

UNCOUNT NOUN

Hay is grass which has been cut and dried to be used as animal food.

He went out with Michael to the barn to help with hay for the cattle.

---

high, higher, highest
hi
/haɪ/

See also **higher**, **hire**.

high

ADJECTIVE

A **high** structure or mountain measures a long distance from the bottom to the top.

...the high walls of the prison.
How high are the walls?
...a 200 foot high crag.

ADJECTIVE OR ADVERB

If something is **high**, it is a long distance above the ground, above sea level, or above a person.

From the high vantage point of the cabin, he could see quite a lot.
The bookshelf was too high for him to reach.

ADJECTIVE

High means great in amount, degree, or intensity.

A high proportion of students live in the St. Louis area.
Her works fetch high prices.

ADJECTIVE

If the quality or standard of something is **high**, it is very good indeed.

...high quality colour photographs.

He said high standards of conduct were essential in the administration of justice.

ADJECTIVE

A **high** position in a profession or society is an important one.

This applies to both the rank and file and high officials.

ADJECTIVE

A **high** sound is close to the top of a range of notes.

Women tend to have high voices.

hi

CONVENTION

You say **'Hi'** when you are greeting someone informally.

'Hi, I'm Harry Benjamin. I guess I'm a little late,' he said.

---

him
hymn, hymns

/hɪm/

him

PRONOUN

You use **him** to refer to a man, boy, or male animal whose identity is already known or who has already been mentioned.

He noticed Miss Leon was still looking at him.
He asked if you'd ring him back when you got in.

hymn

COUNT NOUN

A **hymn** is a Christian song of praise to God.

It is a hymn of celebration of God's greatness and majesty.

---

hoard, hoards, hoarding, hoarded
horde, hordes

/hɔːʳd/

hoard

VERB

To **hoard** something means to store or save it because it is valuable or important to you.

People had started to hoard food and other goods.

COUNT NOUN

A **hoard** is a store of things that are valuable or important to someone.

...a small hoard of coins.
They collect seeds and wild berries, and dig up secret hoards of grain.

horde

COUNT NOUN

A **horde** is a large, rather frightening crowd of people or animals. When **horde** is used in this way, it is usually modified.

Americans reacted as if the country had just been invaded by a horde of criminals.
...hordes of screaming children.

---

horse, horses
hoarse, hoarser, hoarsest

/hɔːʳs/

---

horse

COUNT NOUN

A **horse** is a large animal you can ride or use to pull a vehicle.

He would ride his horse to Calhoun.
The boy fell off the horse and broke his leg.

hoarse

ADJECTIVE

If your voice is **hoarse**, it sounds rough and unclear, usually because you have a sore throat

My voice was a hoarse gurgle, a pitiful, weak whisper.

---

hue, hues
hew, hews, hewing, hewed, hewn

/hjuː/

---

hue

COUNT NOUN

A particular **hue** is a particular colour; a literary word.

The moon grows dimmer and takes on a coppery hue.
...luxurious fabrics woven in glowing autumnal hues.

hew

VERB

To **hew** wood or stone means to cut it roughly; a literary word.

Who would hew the wood and draw the water?
...the rocks we hew for building stone.

I

eye, eyes /a͟ɪ/
aye

I

PRONOUN

I is the word a speaker or writer uses to refer to himself or herself.

I shall be leaving soon.
I see what you mean.
He and I were at school together.

eye

COUNT NOUN

An **eye** is one of the two organs in your face that you see with.

He said it would be five days before my eye healed.

aye

CONVENTION

In some dialects of English, **aye** is used to mean 'yes'.

Aye, it's an isolated spot alright.
'Oh aye, to be sure' said Nora.

---

idle, idler, idlest /a͟ɪdᵊl/
idol, idols

---

idle

ADJECTIVE

Someone who is **idle** is lazy.

It's not true that they are a bunch of idle layabouts. They want to work.

ADJECTIVE

A machine or a factory that is **idle** is not in use.

illicit, elicit

India has 14 idle aircraft on the ground.

idol

COUNT NOUN

An **idol** is someone who is greatly admired or loved by the public.

Hollywood idol Robert De Niro is to star as a real mafia Godfather.

COUNT NOUN

An **idol** is a statue that is worshipped by people who think it is a god.

Jack, painted and garlanded, sat there like an idol.

---

illicit
elicit, elicits, eliciting, elicited

/ɪlɪsɪt/

---

illicit

ADJECTIVE

An **illicit** activity or substance is not allowed by law, or is not acceptable according to the social conventions of a country.

...the illicit transfer abroad of millions of dollars' worth of party funds.
Traffic in illicit drugs was now worth some 500 thousand million dollars a year.

elicit

VERB

If you **elicit** a particular response or a reaction, you do something that makes people respond or react to you in that way.

The government tried to elicit truthful responses by promising that families would not get into trouble.

---

in
inn, inns

/ɪn/

---

in

PREPOSITION

In is a frequently used preposition. You are probably familiar with the uses shown in the examples below. Look in a COBUILD dictionary if you need a fuller explanation of the uses of this word.

We put them away in a big box.
She had a newspaper in her hand.
He taught in a boys' school.
He's never in when I phone.
Nearly everyone dressed in jeans, T-shirts, and scruffy running shoes.

inn

COUNT NOUN

An **inn** is a small hotel or pub.

They stayed in an inn.

---

invade, invades, invading, invaded
inveighed

/ɪnveɪd/

invade

VERB

To **invade** a country or place means to enter it by force or in large numbers.

The first Vikings did not invade Ireland until well after the eighth century.

inveighed

Inveighed is the '-ed' form of the verb 'inveigh'.

VERB

If you say that someone **inveighed against** something, you mean that they criticized it strongly; a formal word.

It was a play that inveighed against gambling.

---

isle, isles
aisle, aisles

/aɪl/

---

aisle

COUNT NOUN

An **aisle** is a long narrow gap that separates blocks of seats in a public building, or rows of shelves in a supermarket.

She grabbed a shopping trolley and charged off down a busy aisle.

SINGULAR NOUN

In a church, the **aisle** is the long, narrow gap that separates the rows of seats and which leads from back to the front of the church. **Aisle**

91

is often used in expressions like 'walking down the aisle' or 'leading someone down the aisle' to refer to the activity of getting married.

Susan visualized her wedding day and saw herself walking down the aisle on her father's arm.

---

jam, jams, jamming, jammed

jamb, jambs

/dʒæm/

---

jam

MASS NOUN

Jam is food made by cooking fruit with sugar.

...pots of raspberry and blackcurrant jam.

COUNT NOUN

A traffic **jam** is a situation when there are so many cars on the road that none of them can move away.

I was stuck in a traffic jam.
The strike has disrupted train and bus services and brought severe jams on the roads.

VERB

To **jam** things into a place means to put so many of them into that place that they are pressed tightly together.

Fridges won't work properly if you jam in so much food that the air can't circulate.
She jams some clothes in a bag and leaves straight away.

VERB

If you **jam** something, or if it **jams**, it becomes fixed in one position and cannot move freely or work properly.

Jam the door open with a brick.
Put the cash through first, otherwise it jams the till.

jamb

COUNT NOUN

A **jamb** is a post that forms the side or top part of a door frame or a window frame.

He supported himself against the door jamb.

key, keys
quay, quays
/ki:/

key

COUNT NOUN

A **key** is an instrument for locking and unlocking something, or for starting a vehicle.

Don't you have a key to this door?
I unlocked the car with Keller's keys and started the engine.

COUNT NOUN

A **key** is a button on a device such as a machine or a musical instrument.

The operator only uses five keys to operate the word-processing facility.
Give your child a chance to strike the piano keys and to experiment with notes.

COUNT NOUN

A **key** is a scale of musical notes.

...an orchestral passage that returns throughout the movement in different keys.

ADJECTIVE

A **key** idea or issue is the main or most important one.

I think income tax is going to be a key issue.
The country's key industries are coal, engineering, and transport.

quay

COUNT NOUN

A **quay** is a landing place for boats.

Your son's motor-yacht is berthed just along the quay.
They had spent the night tied up alongside one of the quays.

knit, knits, knitting, knitted
nit, nits
/nɪt/

knit

VERB

To **knit** means to make something from wool using two long needles.

I thought I might knit her a jumper for her birthday.

ADJECTIVE

A tightly **knit** community is very close and united.

This is a tightly knit community that we have come to know and love.
...a closely knit family.

nit

COUNT NOUN

Nits are the eggs of an insect sometimes found in human hair.

Head lice live on the scalp and stick their eggs, called nits, to the base
of individual hairs.

---

knows
nose, noses

/n**ouz**/

---

knows

VERB

Knows is the '-s' form of the verb 'know'. See **no, know** for an
explanation of the uses of this word.

The duty officer knows the name of every guest here tonight.
Everybody knows of McCullin. He is the war photographer.
He knows Hebrew.

nose

COUNT NOUN

Your **nose** is the part of your face which sticks out above your
mouth, and which you use to breathe and smell with.

My nose is itching.
Johnny punched me on the nose.

COUNT NOUN

The **nose** of a vehicle such as a plane or a car is its front part.

...pictures from a camera in the nose of the plane.
I saw the car's nose appear round the corner.

---

lane, lanes
lain

/l**em**/

---

lane

PROPER NOUN

Lane is often used in the name of streets.

...268 Spendmore Lane.

A year later we moved from Richland Lane.

COUNT NOUN

A **lane** is a narrow road in the country.

The villa was an old building a little way down a lane.

COUNT NOUN

A **lane** is one of the narrow sections of a wide road, a race course, or a swimming pool.

He dodged from lane to lane on the motorway at speeds of up to 114mph.

lain

Lain is the past participle form of some meanings of the verb 'lie'.

VERB

If you say that someone has **lain** somewhere, you mean that they rested there in a flat or horizontal position.

She has lain sleeping in the hotel room in Livingstone.
The child had just lain in the heart of the forest paralyzed with fear.

VERB

If you say that an object has **lain** in a particular place, you mean that it rested in a flat position in that place.

His hand, which had lain only lightly on hers, now gripped it.
Bricks should always be lain on edge lengthwise.

---

laps

lapse, lapses, lapsing, lapsed

/l<u>æ</u>ps/

---

laps

Laps is the plural form of the noun 'lap' and the '-s' form of the verb 'lap'.

COUNT NOUN

If you talk about people's **laps**, you are talking about the flat area formed by their thighs when they sit down.

They folded their hands in their laps.

COUNT NOUN

Laps are circuits of a race-track.

Heavy rain stopped the race after 24 laps.

VERB

When water **laps** against something such as the shore or the side of a boat, it touches it so that it makes a noise; a literary use.

The sea softly laps the sand.

● **Laps** also occurs in the '-s' form of the phrasal verb **lap up**.

lapse

SINGULAR NOUN

A **lapse** is a period of time that is long enough for a situation to change. When **lapse** is used in this way, it is usually modified.

After a certain lapse of time, it would be safe for Daisy to return.
He was not conscious of the time lapse.

COUNT NOUN

A **lapse** is an instance of bad behaviour by someone who usually behaves well.

I intended to make up for this lapse of manners at the next party.

COUNT NOUN

If you have a **lapse** of memory or concentration, you forget about something or fail to concentrate on something.

A lapse of memory led to the KGB leadership's failure.

VERB

If you allow something such as a contract to **lapse**, you allow it to end or become invalid and do not renew it.

The union said it would allow the contract to lapse.

VERB

If you **lapse** into a particular type of unacceptable behaviour, you begin to behave in that way.

A depressed person is usually rational, but can lapse into paranoid or deluded thinking.

---

lava
larva, larvae

/lɑːvə/

---

lava

UNCOUNT NOUN

Lava is the hot liquid rock that comes from volcanoes when they erupt.

Latest reports say lava is continuing to flow from the volcano.

larva

COUNT NOUN

A **larva** is an insect at the stage before it becomes an adult.

The larva hatches out and lives in the soil.

---

law, laws
lore
/lɔː/

---

law

VARIABLE NOUN

The **law** is a system of rules that a society develops over a period of time.

You can't hold a demonstration here, it's against the law.
Every company must by law submit its accounts annually.

COUNT NOUN

A **law** is one of the rules in a system of law which deals with a particular type of agreement, relationship, or crime.

Many shops across the country openly flout the law which prohibits trading on Sunday.

UNCOUNT NOUN

Law is used to refer to professions related to the law.

Identify a field in which the teenager might want to work someday, for example, law.

lore

UNCOUNT NOUN

The **lore** of a particular culture or country is its traditional stories and history.

Their duty was to make sure that the lore was not forgotten.

---

lays
laze, lazes, lazing, lazed
/leɪz/

---

lays

Lays is the '-s' form of the verb 'lay'.

VERB

If someone **lays** something somewhere, they place it there gently.

The birth attendant then lays the baby on the mother's abdomen.
Phil carefully lays out a row of eight boxes.

leak, leek

If someone **lays** the table, they prepare it so that it is ready for people to eat a meal at.

He does the shopping, does the cooking, and lays the table.

laze

VERB

To **laze** means to relax and do nothing.

Just laze the day away, sitting in your deckchair.

● **Laze** also occurs in the following phrasal verbs: **laze about; laze around.**

---

leak, leaks, leaking, leaked
leek, leeks

/li:k/

---

leak

VERB

If a container or covering **leaks**, it allows a substance to escape through a hole or crack.

Their tent began to leak.
The repaired fuel tank was found to leak.

VERB

If substances **leak**, they escape from the container they are in through a hole or crack.

Oil is continuing to leak from the ship.
Simply stated, the earth leaks carbon dioxide out through its cracks.

COUNT NOUN

A **leak** is a hole or crack through which a substance escapes from its container.

Check for leaks in gutters and pipes first.

VERB

To **leak** secret information means to reveal it.

Protection won't apply any longer to government employees who leak information.
News of de Graef's discovery had begun to leak out.

COUNT NOUN

A **leak** of secret information is the public exposure of it.

The leak could not have come at a worse time for the Commission.

There were also leaks to the Scottish newspapers spreading the rumour.

● **Leak** also occurs in the phrasal verb **leak out**.

leek

COUNT NOUN

A **leek** is a long thin vegetable, a bit like an onion.

...leek and potato soup.
Wash the leeks under running cold water to remove all the dirt.

---

least
leased

/li:st/

---

least

ADJECTIVE

You use **least** to say that an amount is as small as it can possibly be.

...the thinner animals, who had the least muscle over their bones.
Consumers had the least confidence in the airline industry.

ADVERB

You use **least** to say that something is true to as small an extent or degree as is possible.

They're the ones who need it least.
It is one of the loveliest and least known wines of France.

leased

Leased is the '-ed' form of the verb 'lease'.

VERB

If an object or a building **is leased** to someone, it is rented to them.

They leased a house at Cospoli.

---

led
lead

/led/

---

led

Led is the past tense and past participle form of the verb 'lead'. Note that 'lead' is pronounced /li:d/ when it is a verb.

VERB

If you **led** someone somewhere, you went in front of them and showed them the way.

Alex led me up the stairway.
He led a demonstration through the city.
I was led into the prisoner's dock.

VERB

If a road, path, gate, or door **led** somewhere, it went to that place.

He went where the path led him.
...the doors that led to the yard.

VERB

If someone **led** a race or competition, they were winning it.

Martin Brundle led the race until forced to retire two-thirds of the way through.

VERB

If you **led** a group or organization, you were officially in charge of it.
If you **led** an activity, you started it or guided it.

The Labour Party was led by Wilson.
The rioting was led by students.

lead

UNCOUNT NOUN

Lead is a soft, grey, heavy metal.

Lead is a poison which can produce high blood pressure levels in adults.
...the dark lead spire of the church.

COUNT NOUN

The **lead** in a pencil is the black substance in the middle of it.

Most of us are familar with the element carbon as graphite in pencil lead.

● **Led** also occurs in the past tense forms of the following phrasal verbs: **lead off**; **lead up to**.

---

lent
leant   /lĕnt/

---

lent

Lent is the past tense and past participle form of the verb 'lend'.

VERB

If you **lent** something that you own to someone, you allowed them to use it.

She was reading a book he had lent her.
The person next to me lent me a pair of binoculars.

VERB

If you say that one thing **lent** another thing a particular quality, you mean that it gave the other thing that quality.

The towering oaks lent a sense of timelessness to the old mansion.

leant

Leant is the past tense and past participle form of the verb 'lean'.

VERB

If someone **leant** forward or **leant** backward, they moved their body forward or backward slightly so that they were no longer upright.

He leant forward, head a little bowed, as if in church.

VERB

If someone **leant** against something, they rested against it.

She closed her eyes and leant against the wall.
I managed to make it to the end of the street and leant against some railings.

● **Leant** also occurs in the past tense and past participle forms of the following phrasal verbs: **lean on; lean towards; lean upon.**

---

lesson, lessons
lessen, lessens, lessening, lessened

/les³n/

---

lesson

COUNT NOUN

A **lesson** is a short period of time during which someone is taught something.

Lessons begin at 9.30.
My Mom's going to give me a driving lesson this afternoon.

COUNT NOUN

A **lesson** is an experience you can learn from.

My painful lesson was learning how difficult my patients' lives are.
The financial scare contains lessons for the world economy.

lessen

VERB

To **lessen** something means to make it smaller in degree or amount.

Vitamin C can both prevent and lessen the severity of the common cold.

licence, license

The agreement lessens one of the President's most urgent domestic problems.

---

licence, licences
license, licenses, licensing, licensed /laɪsᵊns/

---

licence

COUNT NOUN

A **licence** is an official document giving you permission to do something.

He took fright and fled from the police because he had no driving licence.
Special licences will be issued to some shops to sell the plant.

See also **license**, below.

license

VERB

To **license** a person, organization, or activity means to give official permission for the person or organization to do something or for the activity to take place. Note that in American English this is spelt 'licence'.

...a new licensing authority with the power to regulate and license vehicles, drivers and operators.
The government held out against pressure to make dog owners license their animals.

---

lightning
lightening /laɪtnɪŋ/

---

lightning

UNCOUNT NOUN

Lightning is the bright flashes of light that you see in the sky during a thunderstorm.

Torrential rain and lightning caused fires, flooding and traffic disruption.

ADJECTIVE

Lightning is used to describe things that happen very quickly or last only a very short time. When **lightning** is used in this way, it always occurs before a noun.

He always gets to the point with lightning speed.

...lightning attacks on the city's defensive walls.

lightening

Lightening is the '-ing' form of the verb 'lighten'.

VERB

If something such as a room or a place is **lightening**, it is becoming less dark.

The sky overhead was lightening now and the rocks and trees across the canyon were visible.

VERB

Lightening a load or an object means making it less heavy.

There is a strong likelihood that by lightening the ship we may float it off the reef at the next high tide.

---

liken, likens, likening, likened
lichen, lichens

/laɪkən/

liken

VERB

If you **liken** one thing **to** another, you say that they are similar.

Rescue crews and investigators liken the destruction to a war-time bombing raid.
Bankers liken these turbulent times to the mid-1970s.

lichen

MASS NOUN

Lichen is a cluster of tiny plants which grows as a green or yellow crust on rocks and trees.

Over 100 species of mosses and lichens have been recorded.

---

links
lynx

/lɪŋks/

---

links

Links is the '-s' form of the verb 'link' and the plural form of the noun 'link'.

VERB

If something **links** two or more people or things, it creates a relationship between them.

The complicated social network that links the people of the outlying villages.

VERB

If something **links** two or more people or things, it creates a physical connection between them.

...the main railway line which links Bedford to the north of London.

COUNT NOUN

Links between two or more people or things are relationships or connections between them.

Both have spoken optimistically about the prospects for improved economic links.

COUNT NOUN

Links between two or more people or things are physical connections between them.

...the availability of telephone links.
...high-speed rail links.

● **Links** also occurs in the '-s' form of the phrasal verb **link up**.

lynx

COUNT NOUN

A **lynx** is a wild animal similar to a large cat.

...the Iberian lynx.

---

loan, loans, loaning, loaned
lone

/lo͞on/

---

loan

COUNT NOUN

A **loan** is a sum of money which someone borrows from a person or organization.

The finance ministry is refusing to approve a 500 million dollar loan which had been promised to Poland.
The loan will now be repaid over twelve years.

SINGULAR NOUN

If someone gives you a **loan** of something, you borrow it from them.

I am in need of the loan of a bike for a week.

VERB

To **loan** something to someone means to lend it to them.

After a time they decided it was probably better to loan the money to the women.

lone

ADJECTIVE

A **lone** person or thing is alone, or is the only one in a particular place.

The fanfare is played by a lone bugler in the tower.

---

loot, loots, looting, looted

lute, lutes

/lu̱:t/

loot

UNCOUNT NOUN

Loot is things or money that people have stolen; an informal word.

There were plenty of stolen radios, videos and other loot on sale.

VERB

To **loot** shops and houses means to steal from them when they are empty during a war or a disaster.

There have been reports of youths taking advantage of the general confusion to loot and steal.

lute

COUNT NOUN

A **lute** is an old-fashioned musical instrument with strings.

...the colourful combination of fiddle, lute and voice.

---

lord, lords

laud, lauds, lauding, lauded

/lo̱:d/

lord

TITLE

In Britain, **Lord** is the title used in front of the names of peers, judges, bishops, and officials of very high rank.

He has been seriously rebuked for criticising the Lord Chief Justice, Lord Lane.
...the Lord Mayor of London.

TITLE

A **lord** is a member of the British nobility.

I think that's Lord Osborne, Lord Bolton's heir.
You will have to live with the lords of Henry's court.

PROPER NOUN

Christians sometimes refer to their God as the **Lord**.

Praise the Lord.

laud

VERB

To **laud** someone means to praise and admire them; a formal word.

His father and associates laud his abilities.

---

made
maid, maids

/me͟ɪd/

---

made

Made is the past tense and the past participle form of the verb 'make'.

VERB

You use **made** to say that someone performed an action. For example, if someone **made** a suggestion, they suggested something.

It does not look good when decisions are made by interested parties.
The announcement was made after a cabinet meeting.

VERB

If something **made** you do something, it forced you to do it. If someone **made** you do something, they forced you to do it.

A sudden noise made Brody jump.
Her parents made their two daughters leave as soon as they could.

VERB

You use **made** to say that someone or something is caused to be a particular thing or to have a particular quality. For example, if something **made** someone happy, it caused them to be happy.

...the Radio 2 breakfast show that made him famous.

VERB

If you **made** something, you produced or constructed it.

He made only a few films each year.
...a mussel stew which is made with cream and white wine.

VERB

If something **is made** of a particular substance, that substance was used to form or construct it.

The houses were made of brick.
...a flute made from bone.

VERB

If you **made** a particular sum of money, you earned that sum of money.

He made a large personal fortune, partly from fees, partly from shrewd investments.

maid

COUNT NOUN

A **maid** is a female servant.

She left the Philippines to work as a maid for a rich family.

---

main, mains
mane, manes

/me̱m/

---

main

ADJECTIVE

The **main** part or feature of something is the largest or the most important one.

Washington's main concern remains arms control.
He didn't finish his main course.
All the main roads in Peking have special lanes <for bicycles>.

COUNT NOUN

A water, gas, or electricity **main** is the pipe or wire that supplies water, gas, or electricity to a house.

A bulldozer had cut a gas main.
...batteries which will be rechargable from the mains.

mane

COUNT NOUN

A **mane** is the long, thick hair that grows on the neck of some animals.

...a mane like a lion's.
...horses with flowing manes and tails.

---

maize
maze, mazes

/m**eɪ**z/

---

maize

UNCOUNT NOUN

Maize is a tall plant which produces corn.

Maize grows very well in Tanzania, Zambia and Zimbabwe.

maze

COUNT NOUN

A **maze** is a system of complicated passages.

They would immediately disappear into the maze of back alleys.
...a maze of interconnected pipes.

---

male, males
mail, mails, mailing, mailed

/m**eɪ**l/

---

male

COUNT NOUN

A **male** is a person or animal of the sex unable to lay eggs or give birth.

Female turkeys started laying fertile eggs without ever having seen a male.
Have a look at the platform at the conference and you will find it dominated by white males.

ADJECTIVE

A **male** person or animal is of the sex unable to lay eggs or give birth.

We now have male nurses.
Your boss is almost certainly there because he is male.

ADJECTIVE

Male is used to describe things which concern or affect men rather than women.

There is only marginal improvement in male employment in 1995
...male attitudes.

mail

UNCOUNT NOUN

Mail is letters and parcels delivered by the Post Office.

Every year, each adult receives about 60 pieces of unsolicited mail.

SINGULAR NOUN

The **mail** is the system used by the Post Office for collecting and delivering letters and parcels.

...a 20-year correspondence by mail.
This will take four or five days, depending on the mail.

VERB

To **mail** something to someone means to post it to them.

Put your reply in a plain envelope and mail it to the address below.

---

manner, manners
manor, manors

/mænəʳ/

---

manner

SINGULAR NOUN

Your **manner** is the way you behave. When **manner** is used in this way, it is usually modified.

Behind her hesitant manner and nervous laughter lies a determined soul.

SINGULAR NOUN

The **manner** in which you do something is the way you do it. When **manner** is used in this way, it is usually modified.

The nation still commands considerable sympathy for its cause, but perhaps rather less for the manner in which it is pursuing it.

PLURAL NOUN

If someone has **good manners**, they behave in a polite way. If someone has **bad manners**, they behave in an impolite way.

I do think we should all strive to have good manners.
...etiquette books like Debrett's guides to manners.

manor

COUNT NOUN

A **manor** is a large house in the country.

Mapledurham House is an Elizabethan manor inhabited by the Blount family.

109

---

marshal, marshals, marshalling, marshalled
martial
/mɑːʳʃəl/

---

marshal

Note that the '-ing' form and the '-ed' form are spelt 'marshaling', 'marshaled' in American English.

VERB

If you **marshal** things or people, you gather them together and organize them.

For eight years he has struggled to marshal a coherent response from divided union leaders.
Several of their leaders are in the region to marshal their forces.

TITLE

A **marshal** is an officer of the highest rank in some armed forces

The defence Minister was promoted last week to the rank of marshal.

COUNT NOUN

In the United States, a **marshal** is a person officially responsible for making people obey the law.

It now seems likely that the settlers will remain until the city marshal arrives to evacuate them.

COUNT NOUN

A **marshal** is an official who helps organize a public event.

Ben Bright, of Australia, was stopped by a marshal in the cycle race for a minor infringement of the regulations.

martial

ADJECTIVE

Martial means relating to soldiers or war; a formal word.

He has finally lifted martial law.
The paper was banned under the martial regime of General Erchad.

ADJECTIVE

Martial arts are techniques of self-defence that come from the Far East.

...wushu, the graceful and precise Chinese martial art.

mat, mats
matt
/mæt/

mat

COUNT NOUN

A **mat** is a small piece of carpet or other thick material that you put on the floor.

...a room furnished with floor-level chairs on a rattan mat.
...a prayer mat.

COUNT NOUN

A **mat** is a small flat piece of cloth, card, or plastic used to protect a table.

She set his food on the mat before him.

matt

ADJECTIVE

A **matt** surface is dull rather than shiny.

...matt black plastic.
...matt white hi-fi systems.

mayor, mayors
mare, mares
/meə^r/

mayor

COUNT NOUN

The **mayor** of a town is the person who has been chosen to lead and represent it for a year.

...the woman likely to become mayor of the US capital.

mare

COUNT NOUN

A **mare** is a female horse.

Within the last month, the deadly virus has killed some 50 mares and foals.

---

mean, means, meaning, meant; meaner, meanest

mien

/miːn/

---

mean

VERB

You ask what words, expressions, or gestures **mean** when you want them to be explained to you. You ask what people **mean** when you are not sure what they are referring to or intending to say.

What does 'imperialism' mean?
I know the guy you mean.

VERB

If you say that one thing will **mean** another, you mean that the first thing shows that the second thing is true or is certain to happen.

A cut in taxes will mean a cut in government spending.

VERB

If you **mean** to do something, you intend to do it. If you **mean** something that you say, you are serious about it.

I'm sorry, I didn't mean to be rude.
I'm going. I mean it.

VERB

Things or people that **mean** a lot to you are very important to you.

Material things don't really mean much to me these days.

ADJECTIVE

Someone who is **mean** is unwilling to spend much money or to use much of a particular thing.

I used to be very mean about hot water.
Don't be mean with the tip, he's such a nice young man.

ADJECTIVE

If someone is **mean** to you, they are unkind to you.

She had apologized for being so mean to Rudolph.

COUNT NOUN

In mathematics, the **mean is the average of a set of numbers.**

What you do first is to calculate the mean.

mien

SINGULAR NOUN

Someone's **mien** is their appearance and manner, especially their facial expression; a literary word.

There was assurance in his mien.

---

medal, medals
meddle, meddles, meddling, meddled

/medᵊl/

---

medal

COUNT NOUN

A **medal** is a small metal disc which is given as an award for bravery or as a prize in a sporting event.

...the Distinguished Service Cross and Medal.
He won six gold medals.

meddle

VERB

If you **meddle** in something, you try to influence or change it without being asked; used showing disapproval.

I dare not meddle with my wife's plans.
He alleged that this country meddles in the affairs of Haiti, Cambodia, and Mozambique.

---

meet, meets, meeting, met
meat, meats

/miːt/

---

meet

VERB

When you **meet** someone, you see or are introduced to them for the first time.

He described the woman he would like to meet.
He has a most pleasant and lovable character, and gets on well with all whom he meets.

VERB

When two or more people **meet**, they arrange to be in the same place at the same time in order to do something

They might meet each other in pubs and socialise together.
The Chinese president said Mr Deng still enjoys good health and frequently meets Chinese leaders in private.

VERB

To **meet** a need, condition, or requirement means to fulfil it.

Few employee share schemes meet any of these criteria.
The Indians say the companies failed to meet their obligation to plant new trees.

113

● **Meet** also occurs in the following phrasal verbs: **meet up; meet with.**

meat

MASS NOUN

Meat is the flesh of a dead animal that people cook and eat.

Supplies of food, especially meat, are deteriorating.
...ham and other cooked meats.

---

metal, metals
mettle

/met³l/

---

metal

MASS NOUN

Metal is a hard substance such as iron, steel, copper, or lead.

Bennett makes polished metal boxes.
...little bits of twisted metal.

mettle

SINGULAR NOUN

Mettle is used to talk about the good qualities someone has or how well they can do something. For example, if you **show** your **mettle**, you do something that proves how talented or capable you are; if you are **on** your **mettle**, you are ready to do something as well as you can because you know you are being tested or challenged.

Dean Holdsworth will want to prove his mettle by helping to upstage the champions.

---

mind, minds, minding, minded
mined

/maɪnd/

---

mind

COUNT NOUN

Your **mind** is your ability to think.

They'd been giving her some sort of painkilling drugs which had done something to her mind.
He had an extraordinary mind.

VERB

If you **mind** something, you are annoyed or bothered by it.

Phil was then asked if he would mind taking two stones back to Britain.
I did not mind what I did as long as I was independent.

VERB

You tell someone to **mind** something to warn them to be careful, so that they do not get hurt or damage something.

Mind the ice on the steps as you go.
Mind my specs!

VERB

To **mind** something means to look after it.

He left the bag with me and said, 'Mind that, I'm going to ring my son.'
Parents should screen those who go into their homes to mind children.

mined

Mined is the '-ed' form of the verb 'mine'.

VERB

If a substance **is mined**, it is obtained from the ground by digging deep holes and tunnels.

Coal companies are obliged to pay a tax on every ton of coal mined.
Dr Binns said the depth of the deposits makes it unlikely they could be mined economically in the near future.

ADJECTIVE

An area of land or water that is **mined** has had mines placed in it where they cannot be seen, so that if people attempt to cross the area they may be killed or injured.

The area is heavily mined and four soldiers were killed yesterday in an explosion.

---

miner, miners
minor, minors

/maɪnəʳ/

---

miner

COUNT NOUN

A **miner** is a person who works obtaining minerals or metals from holes or tunnels dug deep into the ground.

His father, an unsuccessful gold miner, died from a fall.

minor

Minor means not very important or serious.

Most flights were on time and any delays were minor.
He said they were in reasonable health apart from a few minor ailments.

A **minor** key is one of the two types of key in which most European music is written.

...Beethoven's C Minor Sonata (Opus 13).

A **minor** is a person who is still legally a child; a formal use.

Britain is the only country in Europe that allows minors to gamble on slot machines.

---

missed
mist, mists

/mɪst/

---

missed

Missed is the '-ed' form of the verb 'miss'.

If someone **missed** a target, they failed to hit or reach it.

We'd keep hitting until one of us missed.
The government admits that investment and employment targets have also been missed.

If something that someone is looking for **is missed**, it is not noticed.

Two babies, looking like piles of rags, were almost missed.

If a person or thing **is missed**, people feel sad because that person or thing is no longer there.

She will be much missed. A memorial service is being held for her at 5pm on Tuesday.

If someone **missed** a bus, train, or plane, they failed to catch it.

The police say he missed his train in Soweto.

Sealink offered to reschedule bookings of passengers who missed their crossing because of hold-ups.

VERB

If someone **missed** an activity or event, they failed to go to it or to take part in it.

I missed a lot of school.
He missed Friday's team practice.

● **Missed** also occurs in the '-ed' form of the phrasal verb **miss out**.

mist

VARIABLE NOUN

Mist consists of many tiny drops of water in the air which stop you from being able to see very far.

...early morning mist lingering in the valleys.

---

moan, moans, moaning, moaned

mown   /moʊn/

---

moan

VERB

If you **moan**, you make a low, miserable noise as if you are unhappy or in pain.

He began to have nightmares, to moan, to cry, and wake up feeling sick.
He had seen them die, watched them writhe and moan from wounds which must lead to death.

VERB

To **moan** means to complain or to speak in a way which shows that you are unhappy.

They also moan that the course is failing to produce the sort of managers they need.
Next week he will doubtless find something different to moan about.

COUNT NOUN

A **moan** is a low, miserable noise.

Each time she moved her leg she let out a moan.

COUNT NOUN

A **moan** is a complaint.

His incessant moan is that if only he could be given the right tools he could get the job done.

117

mown

Mown is the past tense and past participle form of the verb 'mow'. Note that the form 'mowed' is also used.

VERB

When grass **is mown**, it is cut.

A garden of such a size could not be mown by hand.

---

mode, modes
mowed   /moʊd/

---

mode

COUNT NOUN

A **mode** of life or behaviour is a particular way of living or behaving. When **mode** is used in this way, it is always modified.

The bike is the traditional mode of transport for students in the town.
Cornish at that time had been working in a realistic mode.

mowed

Mowed is the '-ed' form of the verb 'mow'. Note that the form 'mown' is also used.

VERB

When grass **is mowed**, it is cut.

Will the lawn be mowed?
...the smell of newly mowed grass.

---

morning, mornings
mourning   /mɔːˈnɪŋ/

---

morning

VARIABLE NOUN

Morning is the part of the day between midnight and noon.

Early on Friday morning there was fighting in the capital.
...a cold autumn morning.
...the daily morning flight to the island.

mourning

Mourning is a noun and the '-ing' form of the verb 'mourn'.

UNCOUNT NOUN

Mourning is behaviour which shows sadness about a person's death.

On his death, President Violeta Chamorro declared two days of national mourning.
He was in mourning for his wife.

VERB

If you are **mourning** someone who has died, you are feeling very sad and thinking about them a lot.

He is mourning a 'perfect woman', the fiancée he recently lost in a drowning accident.

---

mousse, mousses
moose

/mu:s/

---

mousse

MASS NOUN

A **mousse** is a light food made of eggs and cream.

...chocolate mousse.

moose

COUNT NOUN

A **moose** is a large, North American deer. Note that **moose** is both the singular and the plural form.

In Yellowstone Park, I saw elk, moose, bison and pelican.

---

muscle, muscles
mussel, mussels

/mʌsᵊl/

---

muscle

VARIABLE NOUN

A **muscle** is one of the pieces of tissue in your body which is able to become smaller and get bigger again. **Muscles** enable you to move and do things.

Her exertions have unfortunately resulted in a torn shoulder muscle.
Your mouth is mainly composed of muscle.

UNCOUNT NOUN

If a person or organization has **muscle**, they have strength and
power; an informal use.

*...a small British company which could not hope to match Honda's
industrial muscle.*

mussel

COUNT NOUN

A **mussel** is a type of shell fish.

The steak came garnished with mussels and strips of courgettes.

---

muse, muses, musing, mused

mews

/mjuːz/

---

muse

VERB

If you **muse** on something, you think about it slowly and carefully; a
literary use.

I often muse on our place in the universe.
*No wonder Mr Roh has been known to muse that maybe it would be
better if there were two presidents.*

COUNT NOUN

You can refer to something which gives people inspiration and
creative ideas for activities such as writing poetry or music as a
muse; a literary word.

...the muse of music.
In 1923, Miller met the woman who would be his primary muse.

mews

Mews is a noun and the '-s' form of the verb 'mew'.

COUNT NOUN

A **mews** is a yard or street surrounded by houses originally built as
stables. Note that **mews** is both the singular and the plural form.

...the new iron gates outside our mews in London.
...9 Reece Mews, London SW7.

VERB

When a cat **mews**, it makes a soft, high-pitched noise.

The cat mews. 'Shut up', shouts Deborah.

need, needs, needing, needed
knead, kneads, kneading, kneaded

/niːd/

VERB

If you **need** something, you must have it. If you **need** to do something, you must do it.

These animals need food throughout the winter.
Before we answer this question, we need to look briefly at the world environment.
He needs the support of his family.
My wife Jacqueline and I needed some extra cash to buy some furniture.

SINGULAR NOUN

A **need** is a strong feeling that you must have or do something. When **need** is used in this way, it is usually modified.

Ministers agreed that there was a need to make progress.
She felt no need to speak.

PLURAL NOUN

Your **needs** are the things that you need for a satisfactory and comfortable life.

She learned how to provide for her own needs.
The Government would find it hard to meet people's basic needs.

knead

VERB

To **knead** dough means to press and squeeze it before cooking it.

Put the dough on a floured surface and knead it well.
Make a paste by kneading 6 tablespoons of butter with a cup of flour.

new, newer, newest
knew

/njuː/

new

ADJECTIVE

Something that is **new** has been recently made or created.

...smart new houses.
...a new type of bandage that stops major bleeding almost immediately.

ADJECTIVE

New means different from what you have had, done, or experienced before.

Not long after that, he got a new job.
Try and get me her new address.

knew

VERB

Knew is the past tense form of the verb 'know'. See **no, know** for an explanation of the uses of this word.

We had been there before, so we knew what to expect.
Gertler was the only person who knew about the love-affair.
Adam hardly knew a word of Russian.
No one knew how to repair it.
He hardly knew Andrew at college.

---

night, nights
knight, knights   /na͟ɪt/

---

night

VARIABLE NOUN

The **night** is the period in every 24 hours when it is dark outside.

People across the country have spent the night sleeping out of doors.
The rainstorms lasted all night long.
Twenty two of them drove for two days and nights to Addis Ababa.

VARIABLE NOUN

You use **night** to refer to the period of time between the end of the afternoon and midnight.

It's usually at night that people go out for a drink.
Treat yourself to some great nights out at the Alexandra Theatre.

knight

COUNT NOUN

In medieval times, a **knight** was a man of noble birth who served his lord in battle.

..knights in armour.

COUNT NOUN

In modern times, a **knight** is a man who has been given a knighthood.

Bob Geldof was made an honorary knight for his charity work.

---

no

know, knows, knowing, knew   /n<u>ou</u>/

See also **new, knew; knows, nose**.

no

CONVENTION

You use **no** to express different sorts of responses and reactions,
normally to indicate a negative response.

'But you didn't go to sleep?'—'No I stayed awake.'
Oh no, no, no! I'll never let you leave Maltby!
A man was grinning, no, laughing, and waving to him.
A lot of people suddenly find there is no job to go to the next day.
No smoking, please!

know

VERB

Know is a frequently used verb with a number of meanings, all of
which have to do with being aware of or familiar with a particular
person thing. For example, if you **know** a fact, you have it in your
mind and are certain that it is correct; if you **know** a person, you are
familiar with them because you have met them and talked to them.

I'm not letting David know our new address or phone number just in
case he tries to see Rebecca.
'Do you know any English?' she asked the girl.
'Did you know James Partridge well?' 'No. Not well.'
Do you know how to drive?

---

nor

gnaw, gnaws, gnawing, gnawed   /n<u>o:</u>/

---

nor

CONJUNCTION

You can use **nor** after a negative statement to add something else
that the negative statement applies to.

The reports have been neither confirmed nor denied.
My father could neither read nor write.

gnaw

VERB

To **gnaw** at something means to bite at it repeatedly.
Pigs gnaw at the trees' bark.

VERB

If feelings or problems **gnaw at** you, they cause you to keep
worrying.
A vague feeling of apprehension was beginning to gnaw at him .

---

not
knot, knots, knotting, knotted /nɒt/

---

not

NEGATIVE

Not is used to make a negative statement or question. For example,
if you have **not** achieved a particular thing, you have failed to
achieve it; if someone is **not** at home, they are in a place other than
their home.
Unfortunately, I have not been successful.
Ask questions if you do not understand the information.
The details of the deal are not clear.
Not all of Fisher's literary work was successful.

knot

COUNT NOUN

A **knot** is a fastening in something such as a rope or thread.
Sarah licked the end of the thread and tied a knot.

VERB

To **knot** something such as a rope or a thread means to make a
fastening in it.
Push the elastic through and knot the ends together.
Knot the top of the bag securely.

or
ore, ores
oar, oars

/ɔːr/

or

Note that **or** can also be pronounced /ər/. It is pronounced /ɔːr/ when you want to emphasize it (this is known as the strong form), and /ər/ in all other cases (this is known as the weak form).

CONJUNCTION

Or is a frequently used conjunction. You are probably familiar with the uses shown in the examples below. Look in a COBUILD dictionary if you need a fuller explanation of the uses of this word.

What else do you like or dislike about the magazine?
Have you any brothers or sisters?
Students are generally not encouraged to read at home or at school.
Don't put anything plastic in the oven or it will probably start melting.
He can't be that bad, can he, or they wouldn't have allowed him home.

ore

MASS NOUN

Ore is rock or earth from which metal can be obtained.

An agreement has been negotiated to mine and export ore from the Guinean side of the border.
...iron ore deposits.

oar

COUNT NOUN

An **oar** is a long pole with a wide, flat blade at the end which is used for rowing a boat.

The boat had no motor, just a pair of oars.

our
hour, hours

/auər/

See also **ours, hours**.

our

You use **our** to refer to something that belongs to a group of people which includes yourself.

This could change our lives.
It is our jobs and our future at stake.
We were on our own.

hour

COUNT NOUN

An **hour** is a period of sixty minutes.

They had about an hour of talks, but officials declined to give details.
Miners have begun a series of twenty-four hour strikes.

---

ours
hours

/aʊəʳz/

---

ours

PRONOUN

You use **ours** to refer to something that belongs to a group of people which includes yourself.

It is a very different country from ours.
I think I am a caring woman and ours was a loving, communicative marriage.
This is a friend of ours.

hours

COUNT NOUN

Hours is the plural form of the noun 'hour'. See **our, hour** for an explanation of the uses of this word.

He says he worked 12 hours a day, 7 days a week.
They slept for two hours.
...a car alarm going off at all hours of the day and night.

overseas
oversees

/<u>ou</u>və^rs<u>i:</u>z/

overseas

ADJECTIVE OR ADVERB

Overseas means concerning things that happen or exist in foreign
countries across the sea.

The funds had in fact been lodged in overseas accounts.
...tough new regulations which limit the ability of graduates to study
overseas.

ADJECTIVE

Overseas is used to describe people who come from foreign
countries across the sea.

It will aim to stimulate interest in the tourist industry and promote
holidays in Britain for overseas visitors.

oversees

Oversees is the '-s' form of the verb 'oversee'.

VERB

If someone **oversees** an operation or an activity, they make sure
that it is done properly.

The Nature Conservancy Council oversees efforts to preserve the
natural environment.
...the clerk who oversees cathedral finances.

pain, pains
pane, panes

/p<u>ei</u>n/

pain

VARIABLE NOUN

Pain is an unpleasant feeling in part of your body caused by an
illness or an injury.

The old woman had been screaming out in pain.
Police said victims had complained of chest pains.

VARIABLE NOUN

Pain is unhappiness or hardship.

How well I understood the confusion and pain of her parents.
They stressed the short term pains of economic unification as well as
the long term benefits.

127

If someone **takes pains** to do something, they are very careful and try hard to be successful or to do something well.

The trust takes great pains in repairing the buildings.

pane

COUNT NOUN

A **pane** is a flat sheet of glass in a window or a door.

...a pane of frosted glass.

---

pair, pairs
pear, pears /pe__ə__ʳ/
pare, pares, paring, pared

---

pair

COUNT NOUN

You refer to two things as a **pair** when they are the same shape and size and are intended to be used together.

Top-of-the-range training shoes now cost about £100 a pair.
...a pair of Jacobean chairs inherited from his mother.

COUNT NOUN

You use **pair** to refer to certain objects which have two main parts of the same size and shape.

...a powerful pair of binoculars.
...300 pairs of tights.

COUNT NOUN

You can refer to two people as a **pair** when they are standing or walking together, or when they have some kind of relationship with each other.

The pair left Britain in January and were due to return in June.
We worked in pairs.

● **Pair** also occurs in the phrasal verb **pair off**.

pear

COUNT NOUN

A **pear** is a type of green or yellow fruit which grows on trees. It has juicy flesh and is wider at the bottom than it is at the top.

...pear and almond tarts.

pare

VERB

To **pare** something or to **pare** it **down** means to reduce it.

The Association of District Councils issued a statement saying local authorities must pare their budgets.
The luxury tax won't really do much to pare down the budget deficit.

---

palate, palates
pallet, pallets   /ˈpælɪt/
palette, palettes

---

palate

COUNT NOUN

Your **palate** is the top part of the inside of your mouth.
More operations followed, with more jaw and palate cut away.

COUNT NOUN

You can refer to someone's ability to judge the quality of food and wine as their **palate**.
And with not one but four restaurants to choose from, every palate will be satisfied.
He's developed a good palate for French wine since living in France.

pallet

COUNT NOUN

A **pallet** is a rough bed.
The servants normally slept on pallets.

COUNT NOUN

A **pallet** is a wooden platform for stacking goods on.
The warehouse will hold more than 90,000 pallets storing 30 million Easter eggs.

palette

COUNT NOUN

A **palette** is a board used by an artist to mix paint on.
The workbench was littered with brushes and palettes.

pale, paler, palest
pail

/peɪl/

pale

ADJECTIVE

Something that is **pale** is not bright in colour.

The sauce is pale and creamy.
The clouds parted like a curtain, leaving a ceiling of pale blue sky.

ADJECTIVE

If someone looks **pale**, their face is a lighter colour than usual, often because they are ill, frightened, or shocked.

He looks rather pale, but he is calm and relaxed.
She went pale when she heard the news.

pail

COUNT NOUN

A **pail** is a bucket; an old-fashioned word.

...playing in a children's sandpit with a pail and shovel.

---

panda, pandas
pander, panders, pandering, pandered

/pændə/

panda

COUNT NOUN

A **panda** is a large black and white mammal from China.

There are estimated to be about 1,000 pandas left in the wild.

pander

VERB

If you **pander** to someone, you do everything they want; used showing disapproval.

They pander to their children's slightest whim.
...books which don't pander to popular taste.

past
passed

/pɑːst, pæst/

past

SINGULAR NOUN

The **past** is the period of time before the present, and the things that happened during this period.

Drug-dealing in the area has led to violence in the past.
He never discussed his past.

ADJECTIVE

You use **past** to describe things that happened or existed before the present time.

For the past quarter of a century the economy has grown by at least 4 per cent a year.
He refused to answer questions about past business dealings.

CONVENTION

You use **past** when you are telling the time. For example, if it is ten **past** two, it is ten minutes after two o'clock.

He died at twenty-five minutes past ten this morning.
The programme starts at ten past eight.

ADVERB OR PREPOSITION

If you go **past** something, you go near it and then continue until you have gone beyond it.

Thousands of protesters marched past the US embassy in Baghdad this morning.
He drove straight past me.

passed

Passed is the '-ed' form of the verb 'pass'.

VERB

If someone **passed** someone or something, they went past them without stopping.

We passed the New Hotel.
We passed the church and a row of cottages.

VERB

If someone **passed** in a particular direction, they moved in that direction.

They climbed a curving mountain road and passed through a gap in the rocky hills.

The gas is then passed along a pipe.

VERB

If someone **passed** an object to someone, they gave it to them.

The bottle was half empty. 'Want some?' he asked, and passed it over to her.
She passed me her glass.

VERB

When a period of time **has passed**, it has happened and finished.

The time seemed to have passed so quickly.
The first few days passed.

VERB

If someone **passed** a period of time in a particular way, they spent it in that way.

Gary was awake too, and we passed the night talking.
We passed a pleasant afternoon together.

VERB

If someone **passed** an exam or a test, they were succesful in it.

Franklin passed his exams easily.

● **Passed** also occurs in the '-ed' form of the following phrasal verbs:
pass along; pass around; pass away; pass by; pass down; pass on; pass out; pass over; pass round; pass up.

---

paste, pastes, pasting, pasted

paced   /peɪst/

---

paste

VARIABLE NOUN

Paste is a soft mixture which can be spread easily.

It can be produced as a thick paste for painting on trees.
Roughly chop the garlic cloves and grind to a paste with the salt.

VERB

If you **paste** something to a surface, you stick it to that surface using glue.

Within hours rival gangs paste their own posters on top.

paced

Paced is the '-ed' form of the verb 'pace'.

VERB

If someone **paced** a room or a corridor, they walked repeatedly up
and down it.

Disgruntled protestors paced the corridor outside the courtroom.
Calvin paced back and forth across the room.

VERB

The way something **is paced** is the way it is timed or the speed at
which it is done.

He paced the action well, never allowing the intensity to falter.
The adroit mix of comedy and anguish is sensitively paced.

---

pastel, pastels
pastille, pastilles

/pǽstᵊl/

pastel

ADJECTIVE

Pastel colours are pale, light, and soft.
...pastel shades of pink, blue, and brown.

COUNT NOUN

A **pastel** is a colour that is pale, light, and soft.
Our new range of paints includes some new subtle pastels.

pastille

COUNT NOUN

A **pastille** is a small, round sweet, often with a fruit flavour.
...a small tin of throat pastilles.

---

pause, pauses, pausing, paused
pours
paws
pores

/pɔːz/

pause

VERB

If you **pause** while you are speaking or doing something, you stop
for a short time before continuing.

133

pawn, porn

He went on towards the centre of the parkland, wondering whether to pause there for a snack.
He does not pause for breath until he reaches the top floor.

COUNT NOUN

A **pause** is a short interval during an event or activity, or between two events or activities.

There was a pause before someone thought to applaud.

pours

Pours is the '-s' form of the verb 'pour'. See **pour, poor, pore** for examples and an explanation of the uses of this word.

paws

Paws is the plural form of the noun 'paw' and the '-s' form of the verb 'paw'.

COUNT NOUN

The **paws** of an animal such as a dog or a cat are its feet.

The kitten sat down, front paws primly together, and yawned.

VERB

When an animal such as a dog or a cat **paws** at something, it touches it with its feet.

The cat paws the ball playfully.

pores

Pores is the plural form of the noun 'pore' and **pores over** is the '-s' form of the phrasal verb 'pore over'. See **pour, poor, pore** for examples and an explanation of the uses of this word.

---

pawn, pawns, pawning, pawned
porn   /pɔːn/

---

pawn

VERB

If you **pawn** something that you own, you leave it with a pawnbroker, who gives you money for it and who can sell it if you do not pay the money back before a certain time.

I'd prefer to pawn them rather than sell them.

COUNT NOUN

In chess, a **pawn** is the smallest and least valuable playing piece.

I reached down and picked it up, and it was a pawn from a chess set.

COUNT NOUN

If you say that someone is a **pawn** in a particular game, you mean that they are an unimportant person who is being used by other people to achieve a particular thing.

Cuba, he told the masses, will not be a pawn in anybody's game.
They attempt to use him as a pawn in a power-grabbing scheme.

porn

UNCOUNT NOUN

Porn is pornography; an informal word.

...Soho's seedy array of porn shops.

peace
piece, pieces   /piːs/

peace

UNCOUNT NOUN

Peace is a state of quietness and calm.

The peace of this pleasant university city has not been disturbed.

UNCOUNT NOUN

When there is **peace** in a country, it is not involved in a war.

...a practical solution to bring lasting peace.
...the prospects for peace initiatives in the Middle East.

UNCOUNT NOUN

When there is **peace** among a group of people, they live or work together in a friendly way and do not quarrel.

She had done it for the sake of peace in the family.

piece

COUNT NOUN

A **piece** of something is a portion, part, or section of it.

...a piece of bread.
Piece by piece he assembled the rifle.

COUNT NOUN

A **piece** of something is an individual item of it.

The only piece of clothing she bought was a jumper.

...the most important piece of apparatus.

COUNT NOUN

If someone gives you a **piece** of information or a **piece** of advice, they give you some information or advice.

...a valuable piece of information.
...a thoughtful piece of research.

COUNT NOUN

A **piece** is something that is written or created, such as an article, picture, or musical composition.

I'm writing a piece about all the terrible things that can happen to tourists.

● **Piece** also occurs in the phrasal verb **piece together**.

---

peak, peaks, peaking, peaked
peek, peeks, peeking, peeked   /piːk/
pique, piques, piquing, piqued

---

peak

COUNT NOUN

When an amount reaches its **peak**, it reaches its highest level. When something such as someone's career reaches its **peak**, it is at its most successful.

Every few years the population of trout reaches a peak.
...a flourishing career that was at its peak at the time of his death.

VERB

When an amount **peaks**, it reaches its highest level. When a person or their career **peaks**, they are at their most successful.

He forecast that inflation will peak around 10.9 per cent.
Muscle strength peaks at around the age of 30.
His career peaked during the 1970's.

COUNT NOUN

A **peak** is a mountain or the top of a mountain.

Three climbers scaled the Alaskan peak.

peek

VERB

To **peek** at something means to have a quick look at it, often secretly; an informal use.

Then she peeks at you, smiling, and winks.
I peeked round the corner of my curtain and saw this man.

SINGULAR NOUN

If you have a **peek** at something, you have a quick look at it, often secretly; an informal use.

I had a peek in at the van and checked the keys were there.

pique

UNCOUNT NOUN

Pique is a feeling of resentment you have when your pride is hurt.

Rivalry and pique can happen even in the happiest families.

VERB

If something **piques** you, it causes you resentment and hurt.

She impulsively married him to pique her sullen sweetheart.

---

pedal, pedals, pedalling, pedalled
peddle, peddles, peddling, peddled
/ˈpedᵊl/

---

pedal

Note that the '-ing' form and the '-ed' form are spelt 'pedaling', 'pedaled' in American English.

COUNT NOUN

A **pedal** is one of the two bars on a bicycle which you push with your foot to make the bicycle move.

Dismantled bicycles lay among piles of chains and pedals.

COUNT NOUN

A **pedal** is a lever which you operate with your foot.

Anti-lock brakes will not skid no matter how hard a driver presses the pedal.

VERB

To **pedal** a bicycle means to make it move by pushing the pedals with your feet.

The two youths pedalled their bikes across a field.

peddle

VERB

To **peddle** goods means to try to sell them in an unconventional way.

Even his attempts to peddle his paintings proved unsuccessful.

...peddling their jewellery on the streets of Europe.

VERB

To **peddle** something such as drugs or secrets means to sell them illegally.

Do all these young men peddle heroin?
Flynn peddles information to embassies.

---

peel, peels, peeling, peeled
peal, peals, pealing, pealed   /piːl/

---

peel

UNCOUNT NOUN

Peel is the skin of fruit and vegetables.
He doesn't normally eat the peel of the fruit.

VERB

When you **peel** fruit and vegetables, you remove their skins.
Peel the onion and chop it finely.
She sat down in the kitchen and began peeling potatoes.

● **Peel** also occurs in the phrasal verb **peel off**.

peal

VERB

When bells **peal**, they ring.
He pressed the bell push and heard the bell peal within the house.
The church bell was pealing.

COUNT NOUN

A **peal** is a long, loud series of sounds.
She let out a peal of girlish laughter.
...a peal of thunder.

---

peer, peers, peering, peered
pier, piers   /pɪəʳ/

---

peer

VERB

To **peer** at something means to look at it closely.
Major Spender bent over to peer at the paper.
He peers at the neighbours from behind his curtains.

COUNT NOUN

A **peer** is a member of the nobility.

Robes are worn by the sovereign, and by peers.

COUNT NOUN

If someone is your **peer**, they are your equal in age and status.

The volunteers are teenagers themselves. For teenagers who prefer talking to a peer, this is the number to call.
Only her artistic peers comprehended some of her feelings.

pier

COUNT NOUN

A **pier** is a large, long platform which starts on the shore and sticks out into the sea.

...a postcard showing a view of the pier at Worthing.

---

pervade, pervades, pervading, pervaded   /pəʳveɪd/
purveyed

---

pervade

VERB

To **pervade** something means to spread through every part of it; a formal word.

The smell of oil seemed to pervade everything on board.
Fear and unhappiness pervade the whole country.

purveyed

Purveyed is the '-ed' form of the verb 'purvey'.

VERB

If someone **purveyed** something such as information, they told it to people; a formal use.

Indeed, Steinhardt himself at one time purveyed such financial intelligence.

VERB

If someone **purveyed** goods and services, they provided them; a formal use.

She purveyed flowers to appreciative tourists.

phase, phases, phasing, phased
faze, fazes, fazing, fazed /feɪz/

phase

COUNT NOUN

A **phase** is a particular stage in a process or in the development of something.

The strike coincided with the final phase of government plans to sell the state-owned telephone company.
The diet is divided into three phases.

PHRASAL VERB

To **phase** something **in** means to introduce it in stages. To **phase** something **out** means to remove it in stages.

The government now looks certain to phase in its reforms of community care over three years.
...U.S. demands for a firm timetable for phasing out export subsidies.

faze

VERB

To **faze** someone means to upset, disturb, or confuse them.

You get the impression that nothing really fazes her.
I know all about it and I'm not fazed by any of it.

pigeon, pigeons
pidgin, pidgins /pɪdʒɪn/

pigeon

COUNT NOUN

A **pigeon** is a type of large, grey bird which is often seen in towns.

...huge flocks of pigeons.

pidgin

VARIABLE NOUN

A **pidgin** is a language which is a mixture of two other languages. A **pidgin** is not usually anyone's native language, but is used when people who speak different languages communicate with each other.

Pidgin has been a controversial issue in Hawaiian education for 50 years.

They spoke pidgin English.

---

place, places, placing, placed
plaice /pleɪs/

---

place

COUNT NOUN

A **place** is any building, area, town, or country.

The cellar was a very dark place.
...a meeting place.

COUNT NOUN

An object's **place** is the position where it belongs.

She put the book back in its place on the shelf.

COUNT NOUN

Your **place** is the space where you stand or sit, for example, in a queue, on a bus, or at a table.

'Well,' he said, as he took his place at the table, 'what's up?'

COUNT NOUN

Your **place** in a society or organization is your position or role in it in relation to other people.

The Foreign Office supported another view of Britain's place in the world.
Frank felt it was not his place to raise any objection.

COUNT NOUN

Someone's **place** in a competition or scale is their position at the end of a particular stage of the competition or scale.

Carl Prean has retained his place as England's table tennis No 1.
The US leapt from sixth place to second.

VERB

To **place** something somewhere means to put it there.

Peel the pears and place them, stem up, in a saucepan.

plaice

VARIABLE NOUN

A **plaice** is a type of flat sea fish. Note that **plaice** is both the singular and the plural form.

...a whole fillet of plaice.

---

plane, planes, planing, planed
plain, plains;, plainer, plainest

/pl**e**ɪn/

---

plane

COUNT NOUN

A **plane** is a vehicle with wings and engines which can fly.

The plane had flown the equivalent of six times around the world.
We went by plane.
He was killed in a plane crash.

COUNT NOUN

A **plane** is a flat level surface which may be sloping at a particular angle; a technical use.

...a building with angled planes.

COUNT NOUN

A **plane** is a tool for making wood smoother or thinner.

Every time he shoves the plane forward, a slice of wood curls out.

VERB

To **plane** a piece of wood means to make it smoother or thinner using a plane.

Get a carpenter to plane jammed windows.

plain

ADJECTIVE

A **plain** surface or object is entirely one colour and has no pattern or design on it.

They are set against a plain background.
...a plain envelope containing a first-class railway voucher.

ADJECTIVE

Something that is **plain** is simple in style.

She wore a plain white blouse under a tailored jacket.
I enjoy good plain food; nothing fancy.

ADJECTIVE

If a fact or situation is **plain**, it is easy to recognize or understand.

It was plain that Eddie wanted to get back to sleep.
The message for you was quite plain. He intends to be at Canterbury Cathedral.

COUNT NOUN

A **plain** is a large, flat area of land.

Here the land flattens out into a fertile plain stretching to the River Jordan.

---

please, pleases, pleasing, pleased
pleas

/pliːz/

please

CONVENTION

You say **'please'** when you are making a request or a command or accepting an offer and you want to be polite.

Amanda, please show Gwendolen where to hang her coat.
Could I speak to Sue, please?
'Would you like another drink?'—'Yes please.'

VERB

If you do something to **please** someone, you do it in order to make them happy.

He planted a vegetable garden to please the girls.
You're an impossible man to please, Emmanuel.

pleas

Pleas is the plural form of the noun 'plea'.

COUNT NOUN

Pleas are intense, emotional requests for something.

She at last responded to his pleas for help.
There were no further tears or pleas for attention.

COUNT NOUN

In a court of law, **pleas** are the answers people give when they say whether they are guilty or not.

Ball entered pleas of guilty to two attempted murder charges.

---

plum, plums
plumb, plumbs, plumbing, plumbed

/plʌm/

plum

COUNT NOUN

A **plum** is a small sweet fruit with a smooth red or yellow skin and a stone in the middle.

We had a good crop of plums this year.

plumb

PHRASE

To **plumb the depths** of an unpleasant emotion means to experience it to an extreme degree.

They frequently plumb the depths of loneliness and despair.

---

poll, polls
pole, poles /po͞ol/

poll

COUNT NOUN

A **poll** is a survey in which people are asked their opinion about something.

Last year the polls gave the President a 10 to 15 point lead.

pole

COUNT NOUN

A **pole** is a long thin piece of wood or metal.

A flag had to be attached to a high pole.

COUNT NOUN

The **North Pole** and the **South Pole** are the two opposite ends of the earth's axis.

Several photographs showed him standing at the North Pole.

---

populous
populace /pɒpjʊləs/

populous

ADJECTIVE

A **populous** country or area has a lot of people living in it; a formal word.

The Pacific contains the world's most populous country, China.

populace

SINGULAR NOUN

The **populace** of a country is its people; a formal word.

35 per cent of the populace own two cars.

---

pour, pours, pouring, poured

poor; poorer, poorest /pɔːʳ/

pore, pores, poring, pored

See also **pause, pours, paws, pores**.

pour

VERB

To **pour** a liquid means to tip the container it is in so that it flows out of it.

Pour the vegetable oil into a frying pan to a depth of about 1cm.
The man was pouring the red liquid into a cup.
I poured cold water on a towel and mopped my face.

VERB

When liquids or other substances **pour** somewhere, they flow there in large quanitites.

It's cheaper to refix a loose tile now than let rain pour into the loft.
Water from a burst main was pouring out and flowing into the passage.
The liquid poured across the concrete floor.

● **Pour** also occurs in the phrasal verb **pour out**.

poor

Note that **poor** can also be pronounced /pʊəʳ/.

ADJECTIVE

Someone who is **poor** has very little money or few possessions. A **poor** country or area is inhabited by people with very little money or few possessions.

He was one of thirteen children from a poor family.
Many countries in the third world are as poor as they have ever been.

ADJECTIVE

You use **poor** to express your sympathy for someone.

I feel sorry for that poor child.

ADJECTIVE

Something that is **poor** is of a very low standard or is of very bad quality.

The flat was in a poor state of repair.
...poor working conditions.

145

pore

COUNT NOUN

A **pore** is a tiny hole in your skin or on the surface of a plant which allows water to pass through it.

Herbs and minerals added to the bath are easily absorbed through the open pores of the skin.

PHRASAL VERB

To **pore over** a book or information means to examine it carefully.

Your child can spend many happy hours poring over magazines.
I pored over the books with great enthusiasm.

---

practice, practices
practise, practises, practising, practised

/prǽktɪs/

---

practice

COUNT NOUN

You can refer to something that people do regularly, or to the way in which they do it, as a particular **practice**.

Primakov said he would end the practice of using journalists as spies.
We must respect the practices of cultures different from our own.

VARIABLE NOUN

Practice is regular training or exercise in something, or the period of time you spend doing this.

I helped them with their music practice.
Improvement in these skills may be brought about with practice.

COUNT NOUN

A doctor's or lawyer's **practice** is his or her business.

He returned home to work in his father's law practice.
...a doctor with a private practice.

See also **practise**, below.

practise

VERB

If you **practise** something, you keep doing it regularly in order to get better at it. Note that in American English this is spelt 'practice'.

She and her partner still practise for up to three hours every evening.
Lauren practises the piano every day.

VERB

To **practise** something such as a custom or a religion means to take part in the activities associated with it. Note that in American English this is spelt 'practice'.

They have continued to practise their religion for years.

VERB

To **practise** medicine or law means to work as a doctor or lawyer. Note that in American English this is spelt 'practice'.

He went on to study law and to practise it.
Dr Jussek practises holistic medicine.

---

praise, praises, praising, praised

prays   /preɪz/

preys

---

praise

VERB

If you **praise** someone or something, you express approval for their achievements or qualities.

Students also praise their professors for being available after class.
They praise them for keeping their promise.

UNCOUNT NOUN

Praise is what you say or write about someone when you are praising them.

Politicians have to expect criticism as well as praise.

prays

Prays is the '-s' form of the verb 'pray'. See **pray, prey** for examples and an explanation of the uses of this word.

preys

Preys on is the '-s' form of the phrasal verb 'prey on'. See **pray, prey** for examples and an explanation of the uses of this word.

---

pray, prays, praying, prayed
prey, preys, preying, preyed   /preɪ/

See also **praise, prays, preys**.

pray

VERB

When people **pray**, they speak to God in order to give thanks or to ask for help.

The men entered the mosque to pray for forgiveness.
I have prayed so hard that he will live.

prey

UNCOUNT NOUN

An animal's **prey** is the creatures that it hunts for food.

The mole seeks its prey entirely underground.

PHRASAL VERB

If one species of animal **preys on** another species of animal, it hunts it for food.

The peregrine falcon preys on pigeons.

PHRASAL VERB

If a problem **preys on** your mind, it worries you and you keep thinking about it.

Bakker's recent divorce was preying on his mind.
Barton agreed, but the decision preyed on his mind.

---

principle, principles
principal, principals

/prɪnsɪpᵊl/

---

principle

VARIABLE NOUN

A **principle** is a belief that you have about the way you should behave.

She was a woman of principle.
He is reported to have said he would rather shoot himself than compromise his principles.

COUNT NOUN

A **principle** is a general rule or a scientific law about how something happens or works.

The principle is that the welfare of a child should always override the wishes of its parents.

principal

ADJECTIVE

The **principal** person or thing is the most important one.

...the principal character in James Bernard Fagan's play.
...the principal reason for coming.

COUNT NOUN

The **principal** of a school or college is the person in charge of it.

He is principal and founder of the college.

---

prize, prizes, prizing, prized
prise, prises, prising, prised

/praɪz/

---

prize

COUNT NOUN

A **prize** is something of value, such as money or a trophy, which is given to the winner of a game, competition, or contest.

He later won second prize in the Geneva International Saxophone Competition.
What will you do with the prize money?

ADJECTIVE

You use **prize** to describe things that are of very high quality.

His goats ate Desmond's prize roses.
They stole my prize Ming vase.

VERB

If you **prize** something, you value it highly.

Kerr prizes his editorial independence.
Not so very long ago, a gold watch was a prized possession.

prise

VERB

If you **prise** two things apart, you use force to separate them.

You have to prise each page apart.
Prising open the venetian blinds, he looked out into the night.

---

profit profits, profiting, profited
prophet, prophets   /prɒfɪt/

---

profit

VARIABLE NOUN

A **profit** is an amount of money that you gain when you sell
something for more money than you paid for it.

She had bought Jerrico shares and expected to resell them at a profit.
About 75 per cent of small businesses had profits under £50,000.

VERB

If you **profit** from something, you benefit or gain from it.

California profits from energy conservation.

prophet

COUNT NOUN

A **prophet** is a person believed to have been chosen by God to say
the things that God wants to tell people.

...the story of the prophet Joseph and his brothers.

---

programme, programmes
program, programs, programming,   /prəʊgræm/
programmed

---

programme

COUNT NOUN

A **programme** is a series of actions that are planned to be done, or
of events that are planned to take place. When **programme** is used
in this way, it is usually modified. Note that in American English
this is spelt 'program'.

...a programme of modernization.
The management has put together a remarkable programme of
events.

COUNT NOUN

A television or radio **programme** is something that is broadcast on
radio or television. Note that in American English this is spelt
'program'.

He took part in a BBC radio discussion programme.

program

COUNT NOUN

A **program** is a set of instructions that a computer follows.

Computer programs can take care of the mathematics.

VERB

To **program** a computer means to give it a set of instructions which enables it to perform a particular task.

His new job would still require him to program computers.

See also **programme**, above.

---

queue, queues, queueing, queued

cue, cues

/kj<u>u:</u>/

---

queue

Note that 'queueing' can also be spelt 'queuing'.

COUNT NOUN

A **queue** is a line of people or vehicles that are waiting for something.

They waited in the queue to show their passports.
There was a long queue at the bus stop.

VERB

To **queue** or to **queue up** means to stand in a line waiting for something.

I won't queue just to have a drink.
Every fortnight she queues for her cheque at the Social Security.

cue

COUNT NOUN

A **cue** is a signal to do something or for something to happen.

But the conclusion of such a treaty could simply be the cue for the beginning of new talks.

COUNT NOUN

A **cue** is a long thin stick used for playing snooker, billiards, or pool.

He playfully held his broom handle like a pool cue.

---

rain, rains, raining, rained
reign, reigns, reigning, reigned   /r<u>e</u>m/
rein, reins

---

rain

UNCOUNT NOUN

Rain is water that falls from the clouds in small drops.

He would work outside in the rain or snow.
A light rain had begun to fall.

PLURAL NOUN

In countries where rain only falls in certain seasons, this rain is referred to as **the rains**.

Winter is approaching and the rains are expected at any time.

VERB

When it **rains**, water falls from the clouds in small drops.

It's started to rain heavily, so we've headed for the nearest tent.
It's still raining.

● **Rain** also occurs in the following phrasal verbs: **rain down; rain off**.

reign

VERB

When Kings or Queens **reign**, they rule a country.

He wishes to be seen as a king who reigns wisely.
The Emperor Chia Ching reigned from 1522 to 1566.

COUNT NOUN

A King's or a Queen's **reign** is the period during which they rule a country.

The church had been built in the latter half of Queen Victoria's reign.

VERB

You can say that things **reign** when they are the strongest or most noticeable feature of a situation or period of time; a literary use.

To allow anarchy to reign was terrifying.
In the kitchen, chaos reigned.

rein

A **rein** is one of the leather straps used to guide a horse.

Charles grabbed the reins of both horses and led the way back up the mountain.

---

raise, raises, raising, raised
raze, razes, razing, razed
/re**ɪ**z/
rays

---

raise

VERB

If you **raise** something, you move it to a higher position

He tried to raise the window, but the sash cord was broken.
She raises her head to look at me.

VERB

If you **raise** something such as a price or a level, you increase it.

We cannot raise the price of meat above the market price.
The wealthy will suffer if Labour raises the top tax rate to fifty-nine per cent.

VERB

If you **raise** the standard of something, you improve it.

Putting teachers in day nurseries would raise standards.
This charter sets out our commitment to you and to raising our standards.

VERB

If you **raise** your voice, you speak more loudly, often because you are angry.

The verandah door was ajar and I could hear voices raised in argument.

VERB

To **raise** money for a particular cause such as a charity means to get people to donate money to it.

They are raising money for a children's hospital.
They will finance it with funds raised from international investors.

VERB

To **raise** a child means to bring it up.

153

We started living together, and decided to raise a child together.

VERB

To **raise** a particular animal or crop means to breed that animal or grow that crop.

He moved to Petaluma to raise chickens and sheep.

COUNT NOUN

In American English, a **raise** is an increase in your wages or salary; the usual British word is 'rise'.

He hopes to get a raise.

raze

VERB

To **raze** a building, town, or forest, or to **raze it to the ground**, means to completely destroy it.

They came to raze the buildings and slaughter the monks.
They will raze this damned city to the ground.

rays

Rays is the plural form of the noun 'ray'.

COUNT NOUN

Rays are beams of heat or light.

The rays of the sun can be very harmful.
Long, orange-coloured rays of light fell horizontally across the field.

---

raw
roar, roars, roaring, roared

/rɔː/

---

raw

ADJECTIVE

Food that is **raw** has not been cooked.

...beetroot soup with a raw egg broken into it.

ADJECTIVE

A **raw** substance is in its natural state before it has been processed.

The government has banned the export of raw cotton.

ADJECTIVE

If a part of your body is **raw**, it is sore because the skin has been damaged.

Her throat felt raw and her head ached.

ADJECTIVE

If you describe someone as **raw**, you mean that you think they are too inexperienced to know how to behave properly.

I would never put a raw academic in front of a class of senior managers.

roar

VERB

To **roar** means to make a loud noise.

The rain started to teem down, the wind to roar.

COUNT NOUN

A **roar** is a loud noise.

He heard the roar of a plane overhead.

---

read
red
/r<u>e</u>d/

See also **read, reed**.

read

VERB

Read is the past tense and past participle form of the verb 'read'. Note that the base form of the verb is pronounced /r<u>i:</u>d/. See **read, reed** for an explanation of the uses of this word.

Many modern parents have read books about bringing up children.
We read that despatch from Mark Tully.
After the meter has been read, a bill will be sent directly to your home.
He read law at the prestigious Georgetown University Law School.

red

COLOUR

Something that is **red** is the colour of blood or of a ripe tomato.

The room I work in has a dark red floor and white plaster walls.
...a bunch of red roses.

---

read, reads, reading, read
reed, reeds
/r<u>i:</u>d/

See also **read, red**.

read

VERB

When you **read** something that has been written down, you look at written words and symbols and understand them. When you **read** something **to** someone or **read** something **out**, you say written words aloud.

More than a quarter of the world's adult population are unable to read and write.
I have never been able to read music.
Shall I read to you?

VERB

If you **read** a gauge or a meter, you look at it and record the number on it. If a meter or a gauge **reads** a particular amount, it shows that amount.

The thermometer reads 106 degrees in the shade.

● **Read** also occurs in the following phrasal verbs: **read into**; **read up on**.

reed

COUNT NOUN

A **reed** is a type of tall plant that grows in wet areas.
Thick beds of reeds edged the water.

---

rest, rests, resting, rested
wrest, wrests, wresting, wrested

/r<u>e</u>st/

---

rest

SINGULAR NOUN

The **rest** of something is all that remains of it.
She retired at the height of her fame and spent the rest of her life shunning publicity.
It was happening not only in America but throughout the rest of the world.

SINGULAR NOUN

When you have been talking about one member of a group of things or people, you can refer to the all the other members of the group as the **rest**.

The rest of us were allowed to go home.
It was just another grave like all the rest.

VERB

If you **rest**, you do not do anything active for a period of time.

Michael is tired and he has to rest after his long trip.
Stop to relax and rest your muscles.

VARIABLE NOUN

If you have a **rest** or get some **rest**, you do not do anything active for a period of time.

Try to get some rest.

VERB

If one thing **rests** on another thing, it leans or lies in the other thing so that its weight is supported by it.

Her hands rest on my calf.
The gun was resting between his knees.

VERB

If things such as decisions **rest** on a particular thing, they they depend on that thing; a formal use.

The decison was not his, but rested with the House.
The sole responsibility rests on Germany.

wrest

VERB

If you **wrest** something away from someone who is holding it, you take it from them violently.

He wrested the knife from her.

VERB

If you **wrest** something such as power or control **from** someone else, you take it from them with an effort or after a struggle.

He set out to wrest control of education away from the Church.

---

review, reviews, reviewing, reviewed

revue, revues

/rɪvjuː/

---

review

COUNT NOUN

A **review** is an article about a new book or play.

The editor wrote a scathing review of her Selected Poems.

VERB

To **review** a new book or play means to write about it.

Maria reviews books for the Times Literary Supplement.

COUNT NOUN

A **review** of a situation or system is a formal examination of it.

The Health Minister has announced a review of adoption laws.

VERB

To **review** a situation or system means to consider it carefully.

The meeting was called to review the oil supply situation.

revue

COUNT NOUN

A **revue** is a theatrical show, usually featuring songs and sketches about recent events.

There are hundreds of comedy revues going on.

---

right, rights, righting, righted

write, writes, writing, wrote, written   /ra͟ɪt/

rite

See also **wrote, rote.**

right

ADJECTIVE

Something that is **right** is correct.

They remained convinced that they were on the right course.
He was right. I wasn't popular.

ADJECTIVE

If someone is **right** to do something, they are morally justified in doing it.

I'm sure I was right to go.

UNCOUNT NOUN

Right is used to refer to actions that are considered to be morally good and acceptable.

If you do right you prosper; if you do wrong you pay for it with conscience.

COUNT NOUN

If someone has a **right** to do or have something, they are morally or legally entitled to do it or to have it.

She has a right to know what's going on.
Most of the people don't know they have a right to free medicine.

SINGULAR NOUN

The **right** is one of two opposite directions, sides, or positions. **Left** is the opposite of **right**.

The house was about fifty yards down the road, on the right.

VERB

To **right** a wrong means to correct a bad situation or to compensate for it.

There is an opportunity to right a wrong now, if she chooses to take it.
They recognise the urgency of righting the economy.

write

VERB

To **write** means to put words on paper using a pen or pencil.

Write your name clearly on this piece of paper.
He writes in green ink.

VERB

To **write** an artistic work such as a book, poem, or piece of music means to compose it and record it on paper.

In December he started once more to write poems.
I was told it was impossible to make a living by writing books.

● **Write** also occurs in the following phrasal verbs: **write back; write down; write in; write into; write off; write out; write up.**

rite

COUNT NOUN

A **rite** is a traditional ceremony.

She can also be called upon for rites of birth, marriage, and death.

---

ring, rings, ringing, rang, rung
wring, wrings, wringing, wrung

/rɪŋ/

See also **rung, wrung**.

ring

VERB

To **ring** someone or to **ring** them **up** means to telephone them.

She knew that it would be useless to ring the office where Ian worked.

159

Malcolm kept ringing me up.
He said a senior parliamentarian had rung him from Moscow with a request for more details.

VERB

When you **ring** a bell, or when a bell **rings**, it makes a sound.

We can't just walk up and ring the doorbell.
Somewhere a burglar alarm was ringing relentlessly.

COUNT NOUN

A **ring** is the sound made by a bell.

I was startled by a ring at the door.

COUNT NOUN

A **ring** is a small circle of metal worn on your finger as an ornament.

Brian slipped his mother's wedding ring on her finger.
...a diamond ring.

COUNT NOUN

An object or a group of things with the shape of a circle can be referred to as a **ring**.

The sixteen ambassadors seated themselves around a ring of tables.
A ring of people crowded round the speaker.

wring

VERB

To **wring** something means to squeeze water out of it.

He was trying to wring water from his track suit.
She wrings out the cloth.
She sat there wringing the water from her hair.
Diana wrung out a cloth.

VERB

To **wring** your hands means to hold them together and twist them and turn them, usually because you are very upset or worried about something.

He wrings his hands in horror.
The General came to the door, wringing his hands in annoyance.
He looked dazed and wrung his hands.

road, roads
rode
rowed

/r**o͟o**d/

road

COUNT NOUN

A **road** is a long piece of hard ground between two places so that people can drive or ride easily between those places.

The road was blocked by army vehicles.

rode

Rode is the past tense form of the verb 'ride'.

VERB

If someone **rode** a horse, they sat on it and controlled its movements.

He saddled his horse and rode to town.

VERB

If someone **rode** a bicycle or a motor cycle, they sat on it, controlled it, and travelled along on it.

He rode to work on a bicycle.

VERB

If someone **rode** in a vehicle such as a car, they travelled in it.

That afternoon he rode in a jeep to the village.

rowed

Rowed is the '-ed' form of the verb 'row'. Note that **rowed** can also be pronounced /ra͟ud/, and that it has a different meaning when it is pronounced in this way; see **rows**, **rouse**.

VERB

If someone **rowed** a boat, they made it move through water using oars.

During the day time we rowed round the harbour looking at the boats.

roll, rolls, rolling, rolled

role, roles /r<u>ou</u>l/

roll

VERB

To **roll** means to move along a surface by turning over many times.

She rolls the ball across the floor.

VERB

To **roll** something into a ball means to make it into the shape of a ball using your hands.

Picking up a piece of paste, she rolls it into a ball.

COUNT NOUN

A **roll** of paper or cloth is a long piece of it that has been wrapped round itself many times.

He found a roll of bandage in one of the wall cabinets.

COUNT NOUN

A **roll** is a small circular loaf of bread.

I had a roll with my dinner.
He makes his own crispy bread rolls.

● **Roll** also occurs in the following phrasal verbs: **roll back; roll in; roll over; roll up.**

role

COUNT NOUN

A person's **role** is their function or position in a situation or society.

Her role as patron of that charity is to highlight the problems of sufferers.

COUNT NOUN

An actor's **role** in a play or film is the part they play.

The film stars Dirk Bogarde in one of his best roles.

rose, roses

rows /r<u>ou</u>z/

See also **rows, rouse.**

rose

Rose is a noun and the past tense form of the verb 'rise'.

COUNT NOUN

A **rose** is a type of plant with thorns, a beautiful flower, and a pleasant smell.

She bent to pick a red rose.
... a lovely rose garden.

VERB

If something **rose**, it moved upwards.
His little chest rose and fell in quiet, rhythmic breathing.
Smoke rose lazily into the sky.

VERB

If someone **rose**, they stood up.

Hannah finished her drink quickly and rose to her feet.

VERB

If someone **rose** at a particular time, that is the time that they got out of bed.

He rose at five every day.

● **Rose** also occurs in the past tense form of the following phrasal verbs: **rise above**; **rise up.**

rows

Rows is the plural form of the noun 'row' and the '-s' form of the verb 'row'. Note that **rows** can also be pronounced /rauz/, and that it has a different meaning when it is pronounced in this way; see **rows, rouse.**

COUNT NOUN

Rows of people or things are numbers of them arranged in lines.

We all sat on rows of seats in one small room.
Rows of children waited outside the ground.

VERB

If someone **rows** a boat, they make it move through the water using oars.

...the man who rows the boat.

---

rota, rotas
rotor, rotors

/ro͟ʊtə/

---

rota

COUNT NOUN

A **rota** is a list of people who take turns to do a particular job.

They have a rota for sharing 'desk duties'.

rotor

COUNT NOUN

A **rotor** or **rotor blade** of a helicopter is one of the four long pieces of metal on top of it which go round and lift it off the ground.

...the roar of the helicopter engines and rotors.
The rotor blades and propeller began to rotate faster and faster.

---

rough, rougher, roughest
ruff, ruffs

/rʌ͟f/

---

rough

ADJECTIVE

If a surface is **rough**, it is uneven and not smooth.

The ground was rough, tripping my clumsy feet.
The cloth of the uniform was rough against my skin.

ADJECTIVE

If someone is having a **rough** time, they are experiencing a lot of difficult or unpleasant things.

When I was little, I had it pretty rough.

ADJECTIVE

A **rough** calculation, description, or drawing is approximate rather than exact or detailed.

Kenworthy made a rough sketch of the design in his notebook.

ADJECTIVE

You say that people are **rough** when they use too much force to perform a physical activity.

The deputies were probably too rough with him.

ruff

COUNT NOUN

A **ruff** is a strip of cloth or other material with many small folds in it, which was worn around the neck in former times.

. . .an evening dress with an Elizabethan ruff.

COUNT NOUN

A **ruff** is a thick band of feathers or fur around the neck of a bird or animal.

Midge ran her fingers through the cat's white ruff.

---

route, routes
root, roots, rooting, rooted

/ru:t/

---

route

COUNT NOUN

A **route** is a way from one place to another.

The routes to and from France aren't very busy at the moment.

COUNT NOUN

You can refer to a way of achieving something as a **route** to that thing.

The only route to peace and reconciliation was through peaceful negotiation.

root

COUNT NOUN

The **root** of a plant is the part that grows underground.

Plants should have a good root that spreads evenly in all directions.

COUNT NOUN

The **root** of a hair or tooth is the part beneath the skin.

Waxing works by pulling out the hair from the root.

COUNT NOUN

The **root** of something is its original cause or basis.

I sat and talked with her until we got to the root of the problem.

VERB

If you **root** through things, you search through them thoroughly.

If you don't want to root round junk shops and jumble sales, look in the classified advertisements in your local newspaper.

● **Root** also occurs in the phrasal verb **root out**.

rows

rouse, rouses, rousing, roused

/raʊz/

See also **rose, rows**.

rows

Row is the plural form of the noun 'row' and the '-s' form of the verb 'row'. Note that **rows** can also be pronounced /raʊz/, and that it has a different meaning when it is pronounced in this way; see **rose, rows**.

COUNT NOUN

Rows are quarrels or arguments.

We used to have some terrible rows.

VERB

If one person **rows** with another person, they have an argument with them.

She claims she never rows with her husband.

rouse

VERB

To **rouse** someone means to wake them up from their sleep; a formal word.

Steve would rouse me from sleep at 2 am with phone calls.

VERB

If you **rouse** yourself to do something, you make yourself get up and do it.

He couldn't rouse himself to read any more.

VERB

To **rouse** people means to make them feel emotional and excited.

Tom Harkin was the prospective candidate who did more to rouse the crowd there than anybody else.

VERB

To **rouse** an emotion means to cause people to feel that emotion.

She had tried futilely to rouse compassion in him.

rung, rungs
wrung

/rʌŋ/

rung

COUNT NOUN

A **rung** is one of the metal or wooden bars that form the steps of a ladder.

She moved up the ladder, one rung at a time.

COUNT NOUN

A **rung** is a particular level in a system or organization.

...the bottom rung of the managerial ladder.

VERB

Rung is the past participle form of some senses of the verb 'ring'. See **ring, wring** for examples and an explanation of the uses of this word.

wrung

VERB

Wrung is the past tense and past participle form of the verb 'wring'. See **ring, wring** for examples and an explanation of the uses of this word.

sack, sacks, sacking, sacked
sac, sacs

/sæk/

sack

COUNT NOUN

A **sack** is a large bag made of rough material.

A sack of rice should now sell for considerably less.

VERB

To **sack** someone means to dismiss them from their job.

The government agreed not to sack any of the striking workers.

sac

COUNT NOUN

A **sac** is a small part of the body containing something such as air or fluid.

Worker bees returned with full pollen sacs.

---

sale, sales

sail, sails, sailing, sailed

/se<u>ı</u>l/

---

sale

SINGULAR NOUN

The **sale** of goods is the exchange of them for money.

Mr Baker's announcement formalised the sale.
It could have its income doubled by the proceeds of the share sale.

PLURAL NOUN

The **sales** of a product are the quantity that is sold.

Sales of Japanese cars have risen by nearly ten per cent.

COUNT NOUN

A **sale** is an event where things are sold to the person who offers the highest price.

The auctioneers are preparing for an important sale of football memorabilia.
...a two-day coin sale at Glendinings.
The mare cost Sheikh Hamden 440,000 guineas at the horse sales.

COUNT NOUN

A **sale** is an occasion when a shop sells things at less than their normal price.

The sale price is only £9.95.

sail

VERB

If you **sail** somewhere, or if you **sail** a boat or a ship somewhere, you travel across water in a boat or ship.

It will soon be possible to sail all the way from the North Sea to Vienna and the Danube.
The ferry sails six times a week.

COUNT NOUN

A **sail** is a large piece of material attached to the mast of a boat. The wind blows against the sail and moves the boat along.

...a cotton sail edged with ropes.

• **Sail** also occurs in the phrasal verb **sail through**.

---

see, sees, seeing, saw, seen

sea, seas

/s<u>i</u>:/

See also **sees, seas, seize; seen, scene**.

see

VERB

See is a frequently used verb. You are probably familiar with the uses shown in the examples below. Look in a COBUILD dictionary if you need a fuller explanation of the uses of this word.

The place they are most anxious to see is the house where William Shakespeare was born.
This activity has led some of his critics to see Hughes as a nature poet.
I have to apply the law as I see it.
He went to see Williams and accepted the offer.

● **See** also occurs in the following phrasal verbs: **see in; see off; see through; see to**.

sea

VARIABLE NOUN

The **sea** is the salty water that covers a lot of the earth's surface.

...plans for cleaning up pollution in the Baltic Sea.
A year ago, Jo swam out to sea and drowned.

SINGULAR NOUN

A **sea of** people or things is a very large number of them; a literary use.

Kitchener can be seen furiously appealing for volunteers, faced by a sea of eagerly raised hands.

---

seed, seeds, seeding, seeded

cede, cedes, ceding, ceded

/s<u>i</u>:d/

seed

VARIABLE NOUN

A **seed** is the small, hard part of a plant from which a new plant grows.

All these trees were grown from seed.
I'm taking these seeds home to plant.

COUNT NOUN

Seed can be used to refer to the beginning of something. When it is used in this way, it is usually used in the structure '**the seed of** something'.

This friendship could be the seed of an Anglo-German alliance.

VERB

If you **seed** an area of land, you sow seeds on it.

He helped spread the topsoil around the pool and seed the lawn.

cede

VERB

If you **cede** control of something, you give control of it to someone else; a formal word.

The Social Democrats have had to cede the leadership of the current coalition to the Republicans.
The Louisiana colony was ceded to Spain in 1762.

---

seem, seems, seeming, seemed

seam, seams   /siːm/

---

seem

VERB

If something **seems** to happen, or if a particular situation **seems** to exist, you get the impression that it happens or that it exists.

The experiments seem to prove that sugar is good for you.
There don't seem to be many people here today.

VERB

You use **seem** to say that someone or something gives the impression of having a particular quality or feature, although you are not sure that you are correct.

Even minor problems seem important.
They seem incapable of doing the job.

VERB

Seem is used when you are giving your opinion or attitude about something, or asking for someone else's opinion or attitude.

That would seem a sensible thing to do.
It seems to me that you are not really doing all you could.

VERB

If you **can't seem to** be able to do something, you mean that you are unable to do it, although you have tried.

Would you mind cutting this open for me? I can't seem to manage it.
They couldn't seem to understand.

seam

COUNT NOUN

A **seam** is a line of stitches joining two pieces of cloth together.

The seam of her dress was split from armpit to hem.

COUNT NOUN

A **seam** of coal is a long, narrow layer of it underground.

The region boasts the richest seams of coal in the country.

---

seen
scene, scenes

/siːn/

---

seen

VERB

Seen is the past participle form of the verb 'see'. See **see, sea** for an explanation of the uses of this word.

The day before, I had seen an advertisement in the paper.
Smoke was seen coming from the roof.
Earlier, Mr Hurd had seen President Murabak.
He was also seen as a clear favourite to win the job.

scene

COUNT NOUN

The **scene** of an accident or a crime is the place where it happened.

The emergency services, including scientific advisers from the fire service, have gone to the scene.

COUNT NOUN

A particular **scene** is a particular area of activity.

The announcement has been greeted with mixed reaction on the domestic political scene.

COUNT NOUN

A **scene** is one of the parts of a film, play, or book where a series of things happen in a particular place.

The book culminates in a terrible scene when the woman is killed.

COUNT NOUN

You can describe something that you see as a particular **scene**.

Less than an hour later, clouds of tear gas had cleared to reveal a truly nightmarish scene.

sees
seas
/s<u>i:</u>z/
seize, seizes, seizing, seized

sees

VERB

Sees is the '-s' form of the verb 'see'. See **see, sea** for examples and an explanation of the uses of this word.

seas

COUNT NOUN

Seas is the plural form of the noun 'sea'. See **see, sea** for examples and an explanation of the uses of this word.

seize

VERB

To **seize** something means to take hold of it quickly and firmly.

He felt her fingers seize hold of his hand.

VERB

If a group of people **seize** a place, or if they **seize** control of it, they take control of it quickly and suddenly, using force.

He repeated promises that the army doesn't intend to seize power in the country.

● **Seize** also occurs in the phrasal verb **seize up**.

sell, sells, selling, sold
cell, cells
/s<u>e</u>l/

sell

VERB

To **sell** something means to let someone have it in exchange for money.

I will have to sell my house.
A new visitors' centre sells books, gifts and plants.

● **Sell** also occurs in the following phrasal verbs: **sell off; sell out; sell up.**

cell

COUNT NOUN

A **cell** is the smallest part of an animal or plant.

...the tough, crystalline cellulose which makes up plant cell walls.

COUNT NOUN

A **cell** is a small room where a prisoner is locked in a prison.

My visits to her cell had been restricted by the jailer.

---

seller, sellers   /selə^r/
cellar, cellars

---

seller

COUNT NOUN

A **seller** is a person or business that sells something.

'The property', said the seller, 'was worth about £80,000'.
...sellers of car parts and accessories.

cellar

COUNT NOUN

A **cellar** is a room underneath a building.

Off the hall is a door which looks as though it leads down to the cellar.

---

sensor, sensors   /sensə^r/
censor, censors, censoring, censored.

---

sensor

COUNT NOUN

A **sensor** is an instrument which reacts to physical conditions.

Sensors detect the temperature and the heater switches on if it falls below a pre-set level.

censor

VERB

To **censor** a text or film means to examine it and cut out any unacceptable parts.

The bishops claimed the right to censor all types of publication.

COUNT NOUN

A **censor** is a person who has been officially appointed to censor texts and films.

sent, cent, scent

The censor had made sure that everyone on screen was fully dressed.

---

sent
cent, cents   /sent/
scent, scents, scenting, scented

---

sent

Sent is the past tense and the past participle form of the verb 'send'.
VERB

The most common uses of **sent** have to do with making something go from one place to another. For example, if someone **is sent** to a particular place, they are told to go there; if an object **is sent** to a particular person or place, it is taken and delivered to that person or place, usually by a special service such as the post.

The Queen has sent messages of sympathy to their families.
A lot of the food is put into containers and sent abroad.
The Foreign Minister was sent to Brussels.
The noise sent them racing towards the bush.
Cunningham sent a signal to all his ships at sea.

● **Sent** also occurs in the past tense and past participle forms of the following phrasal verbs: **send for; send in; send off; send out; send up.**

cent

COUNT NOUN

In some currencies, a **cent** is a coin of low value.

They were able to buy very good wines at fifty cents a bottle.

scent

COUNT NOUN

A **scent** is a pleasant smell.

Already the air was fragrant with the scent of roses and lilies.

MASS NOUN

Scent is a liquid that some women put on their skin to make them smell nice.

..a bottle of scent.
Several new scents hit the shops this autumn.

VERB

To **scent** something means to make it smell pleasant.

The fragrances of linden and honeysuckle scent the air.

VERB

To **scent** a person or animal means to become aware of them by smelling them.

...dogs which scent the hidden birds.

---

shake, shakes, shaking, shook
sheikh, sheikhs
/ʃeɪk/

---

shake

VERB

If you **shake** someone or something, or if they **shake**, they move quickly backwards and forwards or up and down.

If the fruit is mature, you can shake the tree's branches to cause it to drop.
Sometimes his whole body would shake uncontrollably.

VERB

If events **shake** you, they shock and upset you.

He says the growth of youth violence shakes him to the core.

● **Shake** also occurs in the following phrasal verbs: **shake off; shake up,**

sheikh

COUNT NOUN

A **sheikh** is an Arab chief or ruler.

The Ambassador said the meeting with the Sheikh was part of a series that he has been having.

---

sheer
shear, shears, shearing, sheared
/ʃɪər/

---

sheer

ADJECTIVE

Sheer is used to emphasize the word it describes.

My immediate reaction is sheer delight.
The reality of racing is sheer hard work. It is often dangerous too.

ADJECTIVE

A **sheer** slope is very steep.

When you reach the cliff edge it is a sheer drop to the sea.

ADJECTIVE

Sheer material is very thin and almost transparent.

...a sheer silk negligee.

shear

VERB

To **shear** a sheep means to cut off its wool.

It is costing more to shear the sheep than farmers can earn from selling the wool.

---

shoe, shoes
shoo, shoos, shooing, shooed

/ʃuː/

---

shoe

COUNT NOUN

A **shoe** is an object you wear on your foot, usually over a sock.

She needs a new pair of shoes.
...shoe polish.

shoo

VERB

If you **shoo** an animal or person somewhere, you make them go there by waving your hands or arms at them.

Karima shooed him out of the hut.

CONVENTION

You say **'shoo!'** to an animal to make it go away.

Mimi clapped her hands. 'Shoo, bird, shoo!'

---

shoot, shoots, shooting, shot
chute, chutes

/ʃuːt/

---

shoot

VERB

To **shoot** means to fire a bullet from a gun. To **shoot** a person or animal means to kill or injure them by firing a bullet at them from a gun.

The men were armed and ready to shoot.
'Don't shoot!' he shouted.
His elder brother returns and shoots two of the men dead.

COUNT NOUN

A **shoot** is a plant that is beginning to grow, or part of a plant such as a stem that is beginning to grow.

If you have shoots growing where they're not wanted, pull them out.

● **Shoot** also occurs in the following phrasal verbs: **shoot down**; **shoot up**.

chute

COUNT NOUN

A **chute** is a steep narrow slope which things can slide down.

Their bags wobbled and slid down the chute.

---

side, sides   /sa͟ɪd/
sighed

---

side

COUNT NOUN

The **side** of something is a position to the left or right of it.

What it does is help the left-hand side of the heart pump blood around the body.
Attached to each side of the machine is a large plough.
The bomb was packed into a drain at the side of the road.

COUNT NOUN

A particular **side** of something is one aspect of it.

But there is another side to the situation.
He might well be seeking to present a more attractive side of his nature.

COUNT NOUN

A **side** is one of two or more groups of people involved in something such as an argument, war, or game.

The military government said that the attempted coup had been put down without casualties on either side.

sighed

Sighed is the '-ed' form of the verb 'sigh'.

VERB

If you **sighed**, you let out a deep breath as a way of expressing feelings such as disappointment, tiredness, or pleasure.

We all sighed resignedly.
'Thank goodness for that, then,' I sighed with relief.

---

sight, sights, sighting, sighted
site, sites, siting, sited /saɪt/
cite, cites, citing, cited

See also **sighted, sited, cited**.

sight

UNCOUNT NOUN

Sight is the ability to see.

She is flying out to Russia for an operation her parents hope will save her sight.

COUNT NOUN

A **sight** is something that you see.

This was the most encouraging sight I'd seen all day.

PLURAL NOUN

The **sights** are interesting places that are often visited by tourists.

Starting in Bangkok, we see the city's famous sights before flying to Rangoon.

VERB

To **sight** something means to see it suddenly or for the first time.

He was the first man to sight the enemy.
After many days without sighting a sail, he saw another small craft heading the opposite way.

site

COUNT NOUN

A **site** is a piece of ground used for a particular purpose.

Finding a site for a toxic waste dump can be a tricky and controversial business.

He had worked on building sites as a labourer.

VERB

If something **is sited** in a particular place or position, it is placed there.

The soap factory was sited in the impoverished outskirts of Glasgow.

cite

VERB

To **cite** something means to quote it or mention it, especially as an example or proof of what you are saying.

The authors cite three facts which, in their view, make a future war likely.
Boren cites polls that show a large majority of voters favoring spending limits.

---

sighted
sited   /saɪtɪd/
cited

---

sighted

ADJECTIVE

Sighted people are not blind.

The fact is blindness hadn't stopped the children doing many of the things that sighted children enjoy.

VERB

Sighted is the '-ed' form of the verb 'sight'. See **sight, site, cite** for examples and an explanation of the uses of this word.

sited

VERB

Sited is the '-ed' form of the verb 'site'. See **sight, site, cite** for examples and an explanation of the uses of this word.

cited

VERB

Cited is the '-ed' form of the verb 'cite'. See **sight, site, cite** for examples and an explanation of the uses of this word.

---

size, sizes
sighs /s<u>aɪ</u>z/

---

size

UNCOUNT NOUN

The **size** of something is how big or small it is.

The only question at issue seemed to be the size of the winning margin.

COUNT NOUN

A **size** is one of a series of graded measurements, especially for things such as clothes or shoes.

What size shoes do you wear?
Do you have this in a bigger size?

sighs

Sighs is the plural form of the noun 'sigh' and the '-s' form of the verb 'sigh'.

VERB

When someone **sighs**, they let out a deep breath as a way of expressing feelings such as disappointment, tiredness, or pleasure.

Lambert sighs and denies it.
'Oh it was wonderful!' sighs Cooney.

COUNT NOUN

Sighs are deep breaths you let out as a way of expressing feelings such as disappointment, tiredness, or pleasure.

Small talk was met with grunts and tired sighs.
Conservationists are breathing sighs of relief.

---

sleigh, sleighs
slay, slays, slaying, slayed /sl<u>eɪ</u>/

---

sleigh

COUNT NOUN

A **sleigh** is a vehicle which is designed to travel on snow.

...horse-drawn sleighs.

slay

VERB

To **slay** a person or animal means to kill them; a literary word.

He came down from his mount to slay the dragon.

---

so

sew, sews, sewing, sewed, sewn /s<u>ou</u>/

sow, sows, sowing, sowed, sown

---

so

ADVERB OR CONJUNCTION

So is a frequently used adverb and conjunction. You are probably familiar with the uses shown in the examples below. Look in a COBUILD dictionary if you need a fuller explanation of the uses of this word.

Do you have any allergies? If so to what?
Joshua leaned a little closer and so did I.
He could not go on working. So we continued to support him.
We must approach life with an open mind so that we may broaden our understanding.
He was so loyal to you. Why did you go behind his back?

sew

VERB

When you **sew** things together, you join them with a needle and thread.

They teach the children to cook, sew, or knit.
She had sewed rows of lace on her skirts.

● **Sew** also occurs in the phrasal verb **sew up**.

sow

VERB

To **sow** seeds means to plant them in the ground.

You can sow winter wheat in October.
The land was cleared of weeds and sown with grass.

Note that **sow** can also be pronounced /s<u>au</u>/, and that it has a different meaning when it is pronounced in this way; a sow is a female pig.

---

soar, soars, soaring, soared /s<u>ɔː</u>ʳ/

sore, sores

---

soar

VERB

If amounts or prices **soar**, they increase quickly by large amounts.

The government expects the number of jobless to soar.
When his lease expired, his rent soared and he was forced to move out.

VERB

To **soar** in or through the air means to move quickly upwards.

Flames soar into the sky.

VERB

If you say that trees or buildings **soar** above you, you mean that they are very tall; a literary use.

Great trees soar above to cut out most of the light.
The steeple soars skyward and the view from the top is breathtaking.

sore

ADJECTIVE

If a part of your body is **sore**, it is painful or uncomfortable.

Gooch admitted that his left hand is still bruised and sore.
...a sore finger.

COUNT NOUN

A **sore** is a painful and infected place on someone's skin.

Their arms and legs were extremely thin and many had open sores.

ADJECTIVE

If you are **sore**, you are angry or upset about something; used in American English.

He is still sore with the Prime Minister for making his son step down as Chief Minister.

---

some
sum, sums

/sʌm/

---

some

Note that **some** can also be pronounced /səm/. It is pronounced /sʌm/ when you want to emphasize it (this is known as the strong form), and and /səm/ in all other cases (this is known as the weak form).

DETERMINER OR PRONOUN

Some is used to refer to an amount of something or to a number of people or things without saying exactly how much or how many of them there are.

Crack some kernels and add these to the mixture for flavour.
Some were personally abusive, some alleged spite and jealousy.

sum

COUNT NOUN

A **sum** of money is an amount of it.

This gigantic sum should have had a huge impact on financial markets.
The PVC disaster cost a five-figure sum.

COUNT NOUN

A **sum** is a simple calculation.

Invest in a pocket calculator and let it do the sum for you.

---

son, sons
sun

/sʌn/

son

COUNT NOUN

Someone's **son** is their male child.

7 months ago, she gave birth to a son, Michael.

sun

SINGULAR NOUN OR UNCOUNT NOUN

The **sun** is the ball of fire that the Earth and other planets move round, and which provides us with heat and light. You can refer to the light and heat that reach the Earth from it as the **sun**.

He shielded his head from the sun with an old sack.

---

sort, sorts, sorting, sorted
sought

/sɔːt/

---

sort

COUNT NOUN

A particular **sort** of thing is a particular kind or type of that thing.

Today, most of the shipyards have closed, and industries of a different sort flourish on the river banks.
They will have to make some sort of adjustment.

VERB

To **sort** things means to arrange them into groups

He showed me how to harvest and sort the wood to make baskets.

● **Sort** also occurs in the phrasal verb **sort out**.

sought

Sought is the past tense and past participle form of the verb 'seek'.

VERB

If you **sought** something, you looked for it or tried to obtain or achieve it.

At least one other person is still being sought.
Talks with the King himself are sought.

---

soul, **souls**
sole, **soles**

/s<u>ou</u>l/

---

soul

COUNT NOUN

Your **soul** is your mind, character, thoughts, or feelings.

It is very important—it lifts people's spirits, warms their souls, makes them happier.

COUNT NOUN

A person's **soul** is the spiritual part of them believed to still exist after they die.

The thirteenth Dalai Lama had recently died and they were searching for his reincarnated soul.

COUNT NOUN

A person can be referred to as a particular type of **soul**; an old-fashioned use.

A few brave souls are about to try and reverse the trend.

sole

ADJECTIVE

The **sole** thing or person of a particular type is the only one of that type.

'Orlando' will be the sole British entry among the 19 films competing.

ADJECTIVE

If you have **sole** charge or ownership of something, you are the only person who is in charge of it or who owns it.

He said the ANC wanted to establish the sole right to form a
government after apartheid.
Local authorities will have sole responsibility for carrying out 'care
assessments'.

COUNT NOUN

The **sole** of a shoe is the layer of rubber or other material on the
bottom of it.

The material can be used to make tough shoe soles.

---

source, sources
sauce, sauces

/sɔːs/

---

source

COUNT NOUN

The **source** of something is the place, person, or thing you get it
from.

Japan is Indonesia's biggest source of aid and investment.
*Whatever the source, cholera has established a strong foothold in
poorer communities.*

COUNT NOUN

The **source** of a problem or difficulty is the cause of it.

*Drugs were one of the major sources of health problems in adults and
children.*

sauce

MASS NOUN

A **sauce** is a thick liquid which is served with other food.

...poached egg in tomato sauce.
...sauces for spaghetti and other types of pasta.

---

stair, stairs
stare, stares, staring, stared

/steəʳ/

---

stair

COUNT NOUN

A **stair** is one of the steps in a set of stairs.

Not a stair creaks as she makes her way down.

PLURAL NOUN

Stairs are a set of steps inside a building.

Mr Tuerena said he led a group down the stairs, then escaped through an emergency exit.

stare

VERB

If you **stare** at someone or something, you look at them for a long time.

Young audiences are accustomed to television and they're apt to just sit and stare.
He stares for a while into his tepid tea.

COUNT NOUN

A **stare** is a long look at something.

...a sidelong, appraising stare.

---

stake, stakes
steak, steaks   /steɪk/

---

stake

PHRASE

If something is **at stake**, it is being risked and might be lost or damaged.

There's a great deal of money at stake.
His political life is at stake.

VERB

If you **stake** something such as money or your reputation on the result of something, you risk money or your reputation on that result.

He has told colleagues and friends that he is prepared to stake his career on seeing this through.

COUNT NOUN

Your **stake** in something is your share of it.

Now his stake is worth a mere £32,000.

COUNT NOUN

A **stake** is a pointed wooden post.

His boat was fastened by a chain to a stake in the ground.

PLURAL NOUN

The **stakes** involved in a risky action or contest are the things that can be gained or lost.

I'm playing for high stakes.

PLURAL NOUN

You can use **stakes** to refer to something that is considered as a contest. When **stakes** is used in this way, it is always modified.

...the Presidential stakes.
This gives you an advantage in the promotion stakes.

steak

MASS NOUN

Steak is meat or fish without much fat on it.

...a dish of stewed steak.
...fresh Scottish salmon steaks.

---

stalk, stalks, stalking, stalked
stork, storks   /stɔːk/

---

stalk

COUNT NOUN

The **stalk** of a flower, leaf, or fruit is the thin part that joins it to the plant or tree.

Field mushrooms need only wiping or peeling, and the stalk should be removed.

VERB

To **stalk** someone means to follow them, especially quietly or secretly.

....a man armed with a knife stalks a terrified victim.

VERB

If you **stalk** somewhere, you walk there in a stiff, proud, or angry way.

Adela stalks grim-faced upstairs.

stork

COUNT NOUN

A **stork** is a type of bird with a large beak and long legs.

One stork can eat as many as a thousand locusts in one day.

stationery
stationary

/ˈsteɪʃənri/

stationery

UNCOUNT NOUN

Stationery is paper, envelopes, and writing equipment.

He runs his father's stationery and printing shop.

stationary

ADJECTIVE

Something that is **stationary** is not moving.

The tanker is stationary with her lights on to warn other shipping.

stayed
staid

/steɪd/

stayed

Stayed is the '-ed' form of the verb 'stay'.

VERB

If you **stayed** somewhere, you continued to be there and did not move away.

The soil, being so corrosive, had taken all of the timbers away, but each of the rivets stayed in position.
Mr Mundin stayed at his home all day, waiting for the police to arrive.
1932 was not a good year to go looking for a job, so he stayed at Harvard.

VERB

If you **stayed** in a hotel or at someone's house, you lived there for a short time.

They stayed at a friend's beach house.

VERB

If someone or something **stayed** in a particular condition or situation, it remained in that condition or situation.

In the same month France's jobless rate stayed at 9 per cent.
The door stayed shut.

staid

ADJECTIVE

Staid means serious, dull, and rather old-fashioned.

They went to a staid seaside resort.

---

steal, steals, stealing stole
steel, steels, steeling, steeled

/stiːl/

---

steal

VERB

To **steal** something means to take something without permission and without intending to return it.

Some youngsters took advantage of the confusion to loot and steal.
He has been charged with stealing government money.

VERB

If you **steal** somewhere, you move there quietly or cautiously; a literary use.

We could steal up on her.
Simon came stealing out of the shadows.

steel

UNCOUNT NOUN

Steel is a strong metal made mainly from iron and which is used for making things such as bridges, buildings, and cutlery.

...a new pyramid-shaped steel and aluminium building.
...two thin sheets of steel.

VERB

If you **steel yourself** for something difficult or unpleasant, you prepare yourself for it.

Mr Patten should steel himself to make appointments that may enrage the authorities.
The President seems to be steeling himself to try to talk peace with the terrorists yet again.

---

story, stories
storey, storeys

/stɔːri/

---

story

COUNT NOUN

A **story** is a description of imaginary people and events.

Dan, the father in the story, fears he is losing his children.

COUNT NOUN

You can refer to a description or account of real events as a **story**.

Dr John Hardy, a leading specialist on Alzheimer's disease, takes up the story.
Some sad stories are starting to unfold.

storey

COUNT NOUN

A **storey** is one of the different floors or levels in a building.

...a 16-storey apartment house in New York.

---

straight, straighter, straightest

strait, straits

/streɪt/

---

straight

ADJECTIVE OR ADVERB

If something is **straight**, it continues in one direction and does not bend or curve.

The headstones stretch out in straight lines.
These force the roots of the tree seedlings to grow straight.
They both have short, straight, black hair.

ADVERB

If you go **straight** to a place, you go there immediately, without stopping anywhere on the way.

We would have come straight here last night, but we got back too late.
I arrived late, straight from a meeting with my solicitor.

ADJECTIVE

If you are **straight** with someone, you speak to them honestly and frankly.

I don't think she's being completely straight with us.
I hope that he will give me a straight answer.

strait

COUNT NOUN

A **strait** is a narrow strip of sea that joins two larger areas of sea.

...the Strait of Hormuz.

---

straightened
straitened
/ˈstreɪtᵊnd/

---

straightened

Straightened is the '-ed' form of the verb 'straighten'.

VERB

If something that is curved or bent **is straightened**, it is made straight.

They spent the first two days getting the front axle straightened.

● **Straightened** also occurs in the '-ed' form of the phrasal verb **straighten out**.

straitened

ADJECTIVE

If someone is living in **straitened** circumstances, they do not have as much money as they used to and are therefore finding it difficult to manage; a formal word.

He was brought up in straitened circumstances in the forties.

---

style, styles
stile, stiles
/staɪl/

---

style

COUNT NOUN

The **style** of something is the general way it is done or presented.

Fischer took the first game in brilliant style.
It's a fascinating contrast of styles.

VARIABLE NOUN

Someone's **style** is all their general attitudes and usual ways of behaving. When **style** is used in this way, it is always modified.

In characteristic style, he peered over his glasses.

UNCOUNT NOUN

Someone or something that has **style** is smart or elegant.

Both women were rather short and plump, but they had style.

VARIABLE NOUN

The **style** of a product is its design.

swat, swot

The bollards come in two styles and weigh only about 4kg.

stile

COUNT NOUN

A **stile** is a step on either side of a wall that helps you to climb over it.

I set off again, along the path, over the stile, and up the lane.

---

swat, swats, swatting, swatted
swot, swots, swotting, swotted
/swɒt/

---

swat

VERB

If you **swat** an insect, you hit it with a quick, swinging movement.

He lay awake all night, swatting mosquitoes.

swot

COUNT NOUN

If you call someone a **swot**, you mean that they study very hard and have few other interests; an informal use.

I was a bit of a swot at school.

VERB

To **swot** means to study very hard, especially before an examination; an informal use.

How do you find time to swot for exams?

● **Swot** also occurs in the phrasal verb **swot up**.

---

swayed
suede
/sweɪd/

---

swayed

Swayed is the '-ed' form of the verb 'sway'.

VERB

If a person or object **swayed**, it leant or swung from one side to another.

We swayed on the bar stools.
The train swayed round the tight bends.

VERB

If someone **is swayed** by a person or by a piece of information, they are influenced by it.

He is thought to have swayed their decisions with the offer of aid and other financial and technical assistance.

suede

UNCOUNT NOUN

Suede is a type of thin, soft leather.

He insisted that his men needed boots of beige suede.
...a fringed-back suede cowboy shirt.

---

sweet, sweets, sweeter, sweetest
suite, suites

/swiːt/

---

sweet

ADJECTIVE

Food or drink that tastes **sweet** tastes as if it contains a lot of sugar.

These trees produce small fruit, which are very sweet.
...a sickly sweet cream pudding.

COUNT NOUN

A **sweet** is a small piece of food made from sugar or chocolate.

...a bag of sweets.

VARIABLE NOUN

A **sweet** is a dessert served at the end of a meal.

Peter Dixon's five-course set dinners offer choice only of sweets.

ADJECTIVE

A feeling that is **sweet** gives you a great deal of pleasure or satisfaction.

This must be what they mean when they say revenge is sweet.

ADJECTIVE

A person who is **sweet** is pleasant, kind, and gentle.

She really is terrifically pretty and very sweet.
It was sweet of you to think of me.

suite

COUNT NOUN

A **suite** is a set of rooms in a hotel.

We moved to a luxury hotel where I have a suite.

COUNT NOUN

A **suite** is a set of matching furniture, for example for a sitting room or bathroom.

...a three-piece suite.

---

symbol, symbols

cymbal, cymbals

/sɪmbᵊl/

---

symbol

COUNT NOUN

A **symbol** is a design or object that represents a particular thing.

According to native American legend, rainbows are a symbol of union.

COUNT NOUN

A **symbol** of a particular thing is a typical feature of it that has come to represent it.

Around him lay the symbols of the city's battles: wrecked cars and burnt-out artillery pieces.

COUNT NOUN

A **symbol** is a written character used to represent a particular thing.

The chemical symbol for mercury is Hg.

cymbal

COUNT NOUN

A **cymbal** is a musical instrument.

Drums and cymbals beat out a solemn rhythm.

---

tale, tales

tail, tails

/teɪl/

---

tale

COUNT NOUN

A **tale** is a story or an account of an interesting event.

...his new children's tale.
Newspapers had published a stream of racy tales alleging impropriety.

tail

COUNT NOUN

An animal's **tail** is the part of it that extends beyond the end of its body.

The dog wagged its tail.

COUNT NOUN

You can refer to the end or back of something long and thin as its **tail**.

The business jet has a very similar wing with a nick out of the rear edge of each side of the tail.

---

taught
taut

/tɔːt/

---

taught

Taught is the past tense and past participle form of the verb 'teach'.

VERB

If you **taught** someone something, you gave them instructions so that they knew about it or knew how to do it.

He taught English to both Italo Severo and to his daughter.
All British soldiers are taught how to detect a chemical weapons attack.

VERB

If someone is **taught** to behave or think in a particular way, they are persuaded to think or behave in that way.

He has been taught the value of the military.

taut

ADJECTIVE

Something that is **taut** is stretched very tight.

I leant out from the boat, with all my weight on the sheet which kept the sail taut.

ADJECTIVE

A **taut** person or situation is very tense.

As ever, the atmosphere is taut for the penultimate round of the championship.

ADJECTIVE

If a piece of writing or a film is **taut**, it is very concentrated and controlled with no unnecessary or irrelevant details.

Forsyth's intricate plotting remains pleasingly taut.

---

tea, teas

tee, tees   /ti:/

---

tea

MASS NOUN

Tea is a hot drink made with the dried leaves of a particular plant or plants.

They then went across the estate for a cup of tea.
Two teas please.

MASS NOUN

Tea is the chopped dried leaves of particular plants which are used to make tea.

Staples such as bread, rice and tea are already being rationed.
Loose Earl Grey, Darjeeling and Jasmine are the best selling traditional teas.

VARIABLE NOUN

Tea is a light meal eaten in the afternoon or early evening.

He took me out to tea at the Randolph Hotel.

tee

COUNT NOUN

In golf, a **tee** is one of the small, flat areas on the golf course where people start their attempt to get the ball into a particular hole. The small peg used to support the golf ball is also referred to as a **tee**.

At the next tee Ann hit an excellent long drive.
...300 wooden tees.

---

team, teams, teaming, teamed

teem, teems, teeming, teemed   /ti:m/

---

team

COUNT NOUN

A **team** is a group of people who work together or play a particular game together.

Social workers say that they were not interviewed by the inquiry team.

PHRASAL VERB

If you **team up** with someone, you start doing something together.

He and Charles teamed up to advertise the product.

teem

VERB

If a place **teems with** people, there are a lot of people moving around it in a disorganized way.

Mainly, the action occurred in a shadowy, sinister city whose tacky streets teemed with angry demonstrators.

---

tear, tears
tier, tears

/tɪə^r/

---

tear

COUNT NOUN

A **tear** is one of the drops of liquid that come out of your eyes when you cry

She suddenly forgot all her English and helplessly burst into tears.

Note that **tear** can also be pronounced /teə^r/, and that it has a different meaning when it is pronounced in this way; to **tear** something such as a piece of paper means to pull it into two pieces.

tier

COUNT NOUN

A **tier** is one of a series of levels or layers in a structure.
...three tiers of arches carved out of the side of a mountain.

COUNT NOUN

A **tier** is one of the levels in a system or organization.
The new rules replace a two tier system of driving penalties.

---

the
thee

/ði:/

---

the

Note that **the** can also be pronounced /ðə/. It is usually pronounced /ði:/ before a vowel, and when you are emphasizing it, and /ðə/ in other cases.

DETERMINER

The is used before nouns or noun groups to say which particular thing or person you are referring to.

Put the apples in a pan with two tablespoons of water.
He was throwing a spear at the elephant.
This is more theoretical than the others.

thee

PRONOUN

Thee is an old-fashioned, poetic, or religious word for 'you'.

I pray thee hold me excused.

---

their
there

/ðeə^r/

---

their

DETERMINER

Their is used to indicate that something belongs to or relates to people or things that have just been mentioned or whose identity is known.

They said it wasn't their dog.
They have fought for their freedom, and it required great courage.

there

PRONOUN

There is used in front of the verb 'to be' to say whether or not something exists, or to draw attention to it.

There are 800 shore-based schools recognised by the Royal Yachting Association.
There is, however, another view.

ADVERB

There is used to refer to a particular place.

And what about the orbit of the space telescope, will it stay there indefinitely?

---

theirs
there's

/ðeə^{r}z/

---

theirs

POSSESSIVE PRONOUN

Theirs is used to indicate that something belongs or relates to people or things that have just been mentioned or whose identity is known.

It was his fault, not theirs.
They were off to visit a friend of theirs.

there's

There's is the usual spoken form of 'there is'.

There's no kind of inspection service, is there?
There's not going to be enough food for twelve people.

There's is the usual spoken form of 'there has'.

There's been a lot of trouble in the city centre.
There's not been any news from Gerald.

---

through
threw
/θru:/

---

through

PREPOSITION OR ADVERB

Through is a frequently used preposition and adverb. You are probably familiar with the uses shown in the examples below. Look in a COBUILD dictionary if you need a fuller explanation of the uses of this word.

The journey through France the next day was uneventful.
A masked gunman fired through the door of a club in Belfast last night.
It can hardly be through a lack of media attention.
I know what she is going through because I went through it myself.
In short, US banks are going through a painful period of contraction.

threw

Threw is the past tense form of the verb 'throw'.

VERB

If someone **threw** an object or person, they caused it to fall or move through the air, especially suddenly or with a lot of force.

The King threw his hat in the air.
Those who remembered a more terrible earthquake in 1977 threw themselves through windows and off balconies.
As Gunnell crossed the line, she threw her arms up high.

● **Threw** also occurs in the past tense form of the following phrasal verbs: **throw aside; throw away; throw in; throw off; throw out; throw up**.

---

thrown
throne, thrones　　　　　　　　　　/θrəʊn/

---

thrown

Thrown is the past participle form of the verb 'throw'.

VERB

If an object or person **is thrown**, they are caused to fall or move through the air, especially suddenly or with a lot of force.

A crowd pushed up against police lines and missiles were thrown.
She died after suffering a fractured skull when she was thrown against a coffee table by her foster mother.
Stones and bricks were thrown at passing cars.

● **Thrown** also occurs in the past participle form of a number of phrasal verbs. See **through, threw** for a list of them.

throne

COUNT NOUN

A **throne** is a special chair used on important occasions by people such as kings or queens.

...the high, elaborately carved bishop's throne in the cathedral.

SINGULAR NOUN

The position of being King or Queen is sometimes referred to as **the throne**.

Parliament voted overwhelmingly to restore him to the throne.

---

throws
throes　　　　　　　　　　/θrəʊz/

---

throws

Throws is the '-s' form of the verb 'throw'.

VERB

If someone **throws** an object or person, they cause it to fall or move through the air, especially suddenly or with a lot of force.

Look how high he throws the ball up when he's serving!
It puts a length of string round them, knots it and throws the parcel on to the ground.
He throws the sofa across the room.

● **Throws** also occurs in the '-s' form of a number of phrasal verbs. See **through, threw** for a list of them.

throes

PHRASE

If you are doing something that is very complicated, you can say that you are **in the throes of** it; a formal expression.

Greece was in the throes of an election campaign.

---

tick, ticks, ticking, ticked

tic, tics

/tɪk/

---

tick

COUNT NOUN

A **tick** is a written mark used to show something is correct or has been dealt with.

Their answers were perfect, ticks all along the page.

VERB

If you **tick** something that is written on a piece of paper, you put a tick next to it.

Please tick what you want and return the menu by four o'clock.

VERB

When a clock or a watch **ticks**, it makes a regular series of short sounds as it works.

A child's clock ticks slowly in the kitchen.

VERB

If you are trying to find out what **makes** someone **tick**, you are trying to find out what interests or motivates them and makes them behave the way they do.

Marian decided to find out what made Rick tick.

COUNT NOUN

A **tick** is a small creature like a flea.

It has been one of the worst years for ticks which transmit a virus from sheep.

● **Tick** also occurs in the following phrasal verbs: **tick away; tick off; tick over.**

tic

COUNT NOUN

A **tic** is a sudden and uncontrollable movement in someone's face or body.

She developed a tic in her neck.

---

tied
tide

/taɪd/

---

tied

Tied is the '-ed' form of the verb 'tie'.

VERB

If one thing **is tied to** another, it is fastened to the other thing with rope or string.

He was tied to the pillars of the great Philistine temple at Gaza.

VERB

If something such as a piece of string **is tied around** something, it is fastened around it.

The fashion was started by skateboarders who wear bandanas tied around wrists or ankles.

VERB

If one thing **is tied to** another, it is closely linked to the other thing.

Leases on the installations expire next year, and the Manila government has tied a new deal to an increase in American aid.

VERB

If you **are tied to** doing something, you have to do that thing. If you **are tied by** something, you must consider it when you are making important choices or decisions.

Being funded by the local education authority, we are not tied to doing what any particular industry wants.

● **Tied** also occurs in the '-ed' form of the following phrasal verbs: **tie down; tie in with; tie up.**

tide

SINGULAR NOUN

The **tide** is the regular change in the level of the water of the sea on the shore.

You can walk out to the island by causeway at low tide.

SINGULAR NOUN

The **tide** of opinion or fashion is what the majority of people think or do at a particular time.

That speech is seen as his last chance to galvanise his party and turn the electoral tide.

SINGULAR NOUN

You can use **tide** to refer to a significant increase in something unpleasant. When **tide** is used in this way, it is always modified.

...the rising tide of terrorist activity in Europe.

---

time, times
thyme
/ta͟ɪm/

---

time

UNCOUNT NOUN

Time is what we measure in hours, days, and years.

Fear can cause both young animals and human babies to hold their breath for some time.
He is to meet the Indian foreign secretary for talks in ten days time.
He was also left with more time to follow his interest in the arts.

COUNT NOUN

Time is used to refer to a particular point in time, when you are describing what someone does or what is happening then.

At a time of falling pay deals, settlements were bound to be lower.
It's not just Third World countries which are turning to world institutions for help at the present time.

thyme

UNCOUNT NOUN

Thyme is a type of herb used in cooking.

...a tangy tomato and thyme sauce.

---

tire, tires, tiring, tired
tyre, tyres
/ta͟ɪə^r/

---

tire

VERB

If events or activities **tire** you, they make you use up a lot of energy so that you want to rest or sleep.

The run did not seem to tire them at all.
The other men began to tire.

VERB

To **tire of** something means to become bored by it or impatient with it.

They might tire of waiting.
Jay never tires of entertaining friends.

● **Tire** also occurs in the phrasal verb **tire out**.

See also **tyre**, below.

tyre

COUNT NOUN

A **tyre** is a thick ring of rubber, filled with air and fitted around a wheel. Note that this is spelt 'tire' in American English.

The pickets have slashed tyres and caused other damage to the vehicles.

---

to
two
too

/tu:/

---

to

Note that **to** can also be pronounced /tə/ or /tu/. It is pronounced /tu/ before a vowel and /tə/ before a consonant, but is pronounced /tu:/ when you are emphasizing it.

PREPOSITION

To is a frequently used preposition. You are probably familiar with the uses shown in the examples below. Look in a COBUILD dictionary if you need a fuller explanation of the uses of this word.

He has been admitted to a Johannesburg hospital suffering from chest cancer.
Around the streets of Westminster recently, a man has been parading with a placard strapped to his chest.
Mr Warren pointed to the left side of his chest under his arm.
The break was to allow Muslims to go to mosques.
He was warmly physical, with one arm round the neck of the person he was talking to.
The yacht was stuck fast for half an hour until it could be taken for repairs to a badly scratched keel.

too

SENTENCE ADVERB

Too is used when mentioning a person, thing, or aspect of a situation that exists in addition to something indicated by a previous statement.

John said he's coming too.
The troubled minister will have other worries too.
Hugo Young is the most high-minded columnist in the business, and probably the cleverest too.

SUBMODIFIER

Too is used to indicate that there is more of a thing or quality than is pleasant or desirable.

Peking refused to approve the finance, saying it was too costly.
They had to stop the event because it was too dangerous.

two

NUMBER

Two is the number 2.

The two Irishmen were in a blue Ford Sierra.
Two bullets struck their vehicle.

---

toe, toes
tow, tows, towing, towed   /təʊ/

---

toe

COUNT NOUN

Your **toes** are the five moveable parts at the end of each of your feet.

Smith had missed the first match having a bruised toe examined in hospital.
I've got sand between my toes.

tow

VERB

To **tow** a vehicle means to pull it along using another vehicle.

They opened fire as the rescue crew attempted to tow away the damaged train.
The ship tows boats back out to sea.

---

ton, tons
tonne, tonnes

/tʌn/

---

ton

COUNT NOUN

A **ton** is a unit of weight equal to 2,400 pounds in Britain and 2,000 pounds in the United States.

It was a 60 ton barge used to transport iron on Irish lakes and canals.

COUNT NOUN

You can refer to a large amount of something as a **ton** of it.

There always seemed to be tons and tons of money available for weapons.

See also **tonne**, below.

tonne

COUNT NOUN

A **tonne** is a unit of weight equal to 1000 kilograms. Note that **tonne** can also be spelt 'ton'.

The metal is now expected to begin a steady climb towards £450 a tonne by spring.

---

troop, **troops**, trooping, trooped
troupe, troupes

/truːp/

---

troop

PLURAL NOUN

Troops are soldiers, especially when they are in a large, controlled group. The form **troop** is used before other words to refer to things that involve groups of soldiers.

Its troops are under direct NATO high command.
Troop reinforcements are also being sent to the northern edge of the plantation.

COUNT NOUN

A **troop** is a group of soldiers within a cavalry or armoured division.

There is no indication that the heavy pounding on this elite troop has broken their will to fight.

COUNT NOUN

A **troop** of people or animals is a group of them.

...*the First Mayfair Troop of Girl Scouts.*

VERB

If people **troop** somewhere, they walk there in a group.

...*the tourists who troop in during the week.*
We troop into the dining room for lunch.

troupe

COUNT NOUN

A **troupe** is a group of singers, dancers, or actors who work together.

Bands, singers and dance troupes entertained the huge crowd.

tuber, tubers
tuba, tubas   /tjuːbə/

tuber

COUNT NOUN

A **tuber** is the swollen underground stem of some types of plant.

Lift dahlia tubers when the first frost hits the plants.

tuba

COUNT NOUN

A **tuba** is a very large musical instrument made of brass.

The arrangements included a tuba and a french horn.

use
yews   /juːz/
ewes

use

VERB

If you **use** a particular thing, you do something with it in order to do a job or achieve something.

He avoids travelling by car as much as possible, preferring instead to use army planes or helicopters.

207

vain, vein, vane

The new liquid crystals are also easy to use.

VERB

If you **use** a particular word or phrase, you say or write it.

*They argue that the poll tax—or the community charge, to use its
official name—is unfair.*
*Pupils are encouraged to use words even if they can't spell them
correctly.*

● **Use** also occurs in phrasal verb **use up**.

Note that **use** can also be pronounced / juːs /, and that when it is
pronounced in this way it is a noun related to the verb 'use'.

yews

COUNT NOUN

Yews is the plural form of the noun 'yew'. See **you, yew, ewe** for
examples and an explanation of the uses of this word.

ewes

COUNT NOUN

Ewes is the plural form of the noun 'ewe'. See **you, yew, ewe** for
examples and an explanation of the uses of this word.

---

vain, vainer, vainest

vein, veins   /veɪn/

vane, vanes

---

vain

ADJECTIVE

A **vain** attempt or action is unsuccessful. When **vain** is used in this
way, it always occurs before a noun.

*The drafting committee worked through the night in a vain attempt to
finish the special session on schedule.*

PHRASE

If you do something **in vain**, you do not succeed in achieving what
you intended to.

We tried in vain to discover what had happened.
They knew that all their efforts might be in vain.

ADJECTIVE

A **vain** person thinks a lot about their beauty, intelligence, or other
good qualities and is very proud of them; used showing disapproval.

The articles turned Mr Masson's own words against him to draw a portrait of an almost impossibly vain and dishonourable egotist.

vein

COUNT NOUN

A **vein** is one of the many small tubes that carry blood through your body.

His neck veins were swollen.

UNCOUNT NOUN

Something that is written or spoken in a particular **vein** is written or spoken in that style or mood.

Cherubin, on the other hand, strikes me as one of Massenet's finest works in a lighter vein.

vane

COUNT NOUN

A **vane** is a flat blade, for example on a propeller, which is part of the mechanism for using the energy of wind or water or to drive a machine.

...a wind vane on top of the mast.
The vane should be made of a thin piece of wood.

---

veil, veils
vale, vales

/veɪl/

---

veil

COUNT NOUN

A **veil** is a piece of fine, thin cloth that people, especially women, sometimes wear in front of their faces.

She looked at him through her veil.
...flouncy little hats with veils.

SINGULAR NOUN

Veil can be used to refer to something that conceals a particular fact or situation. When **veil** is used in this way, it is usually used in the structure '**a veil of** something'.

The inevitable contradictions this created could be hidden behind a veil of internal secrecy.

vale

COUNT NOUN

A **vale** is a valley; a literary word.

...the vale of Aylesbury.

---

wait, waits, waiting, waited
weight, weights, weighting, weighted

/we͟ɪt/

See also **waited**, **weighted**.

wait

VERB

If you **wait**, you spend some time, usually doing very little, before something happens.

We must hope that they will not have much longer to wait.
They waited for an hour and a half, shouting and waving placards.

COUNT NOUN

A **wait** is a period of time in which you do very little before something happens.

We may be in for a long wait.
Travellers using European airports have become used to long waits at peak holiday times.

● **Wait** also occurs in the phrasal verb **wait up**.

weight

VARIABLE NOUN

The **weight** of something is the amount it weighs.

The sculpture is 14.5 feet in length and 2,800 kilos in weight.
Many people were crushed in their homes as hillsides collapsed under the weight of water.

COUNT NOUN

A **weight** is a metal object which weighs a certain amount.

The smallest one there is the one ounce weight.

VERB

If you **weight** something or **weight** it **down**, you add something heavy to it, usually in order to stop it from moving.

She tried weighting her hems so they didn't blow up in the breeze.
Her little tent was weighted down with kerosene cans filled with sand.

SINGULAR NOUN

If something has **weight**, it has great power or influence, which makes it difficult to contradict or oppose.

The decision will add weight to Britain's case at the forthcoming special conference.

SINGULAR NOUN

If you feel a **weight** of some kind on you, you have a worrying problem or responsibility.

The Government is staggering beneath the weight of terrible economic, social and ethnic problems.

---

waited
weighted

/wˈeɪtɪd/

---

waited

VERB

Waited is the '-ed' form of the verb 'wait'. See **wait, weight** for examples and an explanation of the uses of this word.

weighted

VERB

Weighted is the '-ed' form of the verb 'weight'. See **wait, weight** for examples and an explanation of the uses of this word.

ADJECTIVE

A system that is **weighted** in favour of a person or group is organized so that this person or group has an advantage.

The council argues strongly that immigration procedures are unfairly weighted against the individual applicants.

---

war, wars
wore

/wˈɔːʳ/

---

war

VARIABLE NOUN

A **war** is a period of fighting between two countries.

A lot of people run the risk of being killed or maimed if full-scale war breaks out.

VARIABLE NOUN

You can use **war** to refer to intense competition between countries or organizations. When **war** is used in this way, it is usually modified.

He warned that if the Europeans did not reduce subsidies, a trade war would ensue.

wore

VERB

Wore is the past tense form of the verb 'wear'. See **where, wear, ware** for an explanation of the uses of this word.

80 per cent of competitors at the last Olympics wore Adidas products.
The players wore brown boots.

---

warn, warns, warning, warned

/wɔːʳn/

worn

---

warn

VERB

If you **warn** someone about a possible danger or problem, you make them aware of it by telling them about it.

He took the opportunity to warn again of the threat posed by the crisis to the stability of the region.

VERB

If you **warn** someone not to do something, you advise them not to do it.

The Railway Minister has now announced a national campaign to warn passengers not to carry gas cylinders with them.

● **Warn** also occurs in the phrasal verb **warn off**.

worn

VERB

Worn is the past participle form of the verb 'wear'. See **where, wear, ware** for an explanation of the uses of this word.

A notice on the pub door advises that shoes should be worn at all times.

ADJECTIVE

Something that is **worn** is damaged, weak, or thin because it is old or has been used a lot.

But his people are hungry, their clothes worn.
The worn stone steps of the spiral staircase led up and round.

ADJECTIVE

Someone who is **worn** looks old and tired.

Her husband looks frail and worn, but his spirit appears unbroken.

---

waste, wastes, wasting, wasted
waist, waists   /weɪst/

---

waste

VARIABLE NOUN

Waste is material which has been used and is no longer wanted.

Micro-organisms produce the enzymes which break down the waste.
...the local waste disposal authorities.

VERB

If you **waste** something such as money, time, or energy, you use it on something that is not important or necessary.

The resulting struggle can be extremely costly—especially for economies that can ill afford to waste any resources.
The Government believes that the UK wastes £8 billion a year in inefficient use of energy.

PLURAL NOUN

Wastes are large areas of land where there are very few people, plants, or animals.

...the airid wastes of Siberia.

waist

COUNT NOUN

Your **waist** is the middle part of your body, above your hips.

He kissed her on both cheeks and placed his hands on her waist.
The water was up to their waists.

---

wave, waves, waving, waved
waive, waives, waiving, waived   /weɪv/

---

wave

VERB

If you **wave** or **wave** your hand, you move your hand up and down or from side to side.

His mother waved to him.
Dad likes to wave his hands about while speaking.

VERB

If you **wave** something, you hold it up and move it up and down or from side to side.

One of the men dashed towards them waving his spear.

213

All along the route people applauded and waved flags at them.

COUNT NOUN

A **wave** is a movement of the hand from side to side.

He gave a broad smile and a wave.

COUNT NOUN

A **wave** is a raised mass of water caused by the wind or tide.

The tidal wave struck the region on Tuesday.
The waves crashed on the beach.

COUNT NOUN

A **wave** of a particular feeling or activity is a sudden increase in that feeling or activity.

The city faces a crime wave that seems to get worse daily.

waive

VERB

If you **waive** a rule, you decide not to enforce it.

The programme also waives the conditon that buyers have to have a large cash reserve.
Rules about proper dress may be waived.

VERB

If you **waive** your right to something, you give up your right to have, receive, or do it.

This waives your right to complain about future building work.

---

way, ways
weigh, weighs, weighing, weighed   /we**ɪ**/
whey

See also **wade, weighed**.

way

COUNT NOUN

A **way** of doing something is a thing or series of things that you do in order to achieve a particular result.

...a way of raising funds for the Olympic team.
We must find ways in which we can help the whole of our community.

SINGULAR NOUN

You can refer to the **way** that an action is done to indicate the quality that it has.

I found out the hard way and I'm not going to do it again.
...the courteous way he was received in the White House.

COUNT NOUN

You say that something is the case in the **way** stated when you are referring to an aspect of something or the effect that it has.

The job was changing me in a way that I had not expected.

PLURAL NOUN

The **ways** of a particular person or group of people are their customs or their usual behaviour.

It's up to them to change their ways.
...his funny little ways.

SINGULAR NOUN

The **way** you feel about something is your attitude to it or your opinion of it.

Do you still feel the same way about it?

SINGULAR NOUN

The **way** to a particular place is the route you must take in order to get to it.

A man asked me the way to Tower Bridge.

SINGULAR NOUN

You use **way** in expressions such as **'a long way'** and **'a short way'** to say how far something is.

We're a long way from Cuba.

weigh

VERB

To **weigh** a certain amount means to be that weight.

The locomotives weigh 80 tonnes and are 30 ft long.
Each fruit weighs 5-7lb.

VERB

To **weigh** something means to measure how heavy it is using scales.

Rub the fruit through a sieve, and weigh the pulp.
He weighs the trucks at the port of entry.

VERB

If you **weigh** the different factors in a situation, you consider them carefully.

She weighs the consequences of the different actions.

• **Weigh** also occurs in the following phrasal verbs: **weigh on; weigh upon; weigh up.**

whey

UNCOUNT NOUN

Whey is the watery liquid that is separated from the curds in sour milk, for example when you are making cheese.

...wastes such as milk whey.

---

week, weeks

weak, weaker, weakest

/wiːk/

---

week

VARIABLE NOUN

A **week** is a period of seven days, especially one beginning on a Sunday or Monday.

...the 28th week of pregnancy.
Fighting has been going on for a week.

weak

ADJECTIVE

Weak means lacking strength or energy.

All seven men were now feeling very weak.
Many of the evacuees looked tired and weak.

ADJECTIVE

A person, organization, or system that is **weak** is not very good, powerful, or effective.

In the short term, financially weak agencies should be asked to take out bank guarantees.
Capital investment and demand in the housing sector are weak.
This was a case of very weak circumstantial evidence that has now been further weakened.

---

weighed

wade, wades, wading, waded

/weɪd/

---

weighed

VERB

Weighed is the '-ed' form of the verb 'weigh'. See **way, weigh, whey** for an explanation of the uses of this word.

When she was born she weighed just under 9oz.
The animals will be released after being weighed.
...a delicately worded communique in which he weighed both risks
equally.

wade

VERB

If you **wade** through something such as water or thick vegetation,
you walk through it.

We saw one of them trying to wade across a creek.
You have to wade through the piles of fish and mangoes.

● **Wade** also occurs in the following phrasal verbs: **wade in; wade into.**

---

we'll
wheel, wheels, wheeling, wheeled   /wiːl/
weal, weals

See also **wield, wheeled.**

we'll

We'll is the usual spoken form of 'we will' and 'we shall'.

We'll have to be very careful what we say about this.
We've decided we'll not be coming to the party.

wheel

COUNT NOUN

A **wheel** is a circular object which turns on a rod attached to its
centre.

The train started, its wheels squealing against the metal tracks.
...a full-sized steel-framed bicycle with small wheels.

VERB

To **wheel** or to **wheel round** means to move round in the shape of a
circle or part of a circle.

Its war planes wheel triumphantly over its northern capital.

weal

COUNT NOUN

A **weal** is a mark made on someone's skin by a blow.

He showed reporters weals on his back which he said were the result of
torture.

---

wet, wets, wetting, wetted; wetter, wettest
whet, whets, whetting, whetted
/w<u>e</u>t/

---

wet

Note that the past tense and the past participle form can be **wetted**
or **wet**.

ADJECTIVE

Something that is **wet** is covered in water or another liquid.

I hope you don't get your shoes wet.
Much of the grain was harvested while wet and will simply rot.

VERB

To **wet** something means to cause it to become wet.

A light rain wets the dust in the courtyard.
A column of spray wetted them.

ADJECTIVE

When the weather is **wet**, it is raining.

Officials warn that the weather will turn cold and wet.
She realised how gloomy the country could be on a wet afternoon.

ADJECTIVE

If you describe someone or something as **wet**, you mean that you
find them silly or foolishly sentimental.

Don't be so wet, Charles.

whet

VERB

To **whet** someone's appetite for something means to increase their
desire for it.

The tutor at the college had whetted her appetite for more work.

---

we've
/w<u>i:</u>v/

weave, weaves, weaving, wove

---

we've

We've is the usual spoken form of 'we have'.

We've been able to identify the important regions of this protein.
We've done everything possible to assist the Italian government.

weave

VERB

If you **weave** cloth or a carpet, you make it by crossing threads over and under each other using a machine called a loom.

They weave their own cloth and make their own shoes.

VERB

If you **weave** your way somewhere, you move between and around things as you go there.

...other cars try to weave through the crowds.

whale, whales
wail, wails, wailing, wailed

/we**ɪ**l/

See also **whaling, wailing**.

whale

COUNT NOUN

A **whale** is a very large sea mammal.

The whale died instantly when the harpoon grenade hit its head.

wail

VERB

To **wail** means to cry loudly or to make a sound like crying.

One of the children began to wail.
'I feel responsible for their deaths,' he wails.

COUNT NOUN

A **wail** is a loud crying noise or a noise that sounds like crying.

...the wail of sirens.

whaling
wailing

/we**ɪ**lɪŋ/

whaling

UNCOUNT NOUN

Whaling is the activity of hunting and killing whales.

Norway says it wants to start commercial whaling again.

wailing

VERB

Wailing is the '-ing' form of the verb 'wail'. See **whale, wail** for an explanation of the uses of this word.

. . . a mother wailing for her lost child.
The loud sirens had been wailing persistently for several days.

---

what
watt, watts   /wɒt/

---

what

PRONOUN OR DETERMINER

What is a frequently used pronoun and determiner. You are probably familiar with the uses shown in the examples below. Look in a COBUILD dictionary if you need a fuller explanation of the uses of this word.

What about the Third World countries? Do they have any option?
So what are you going to do?
What does it look like, this thing?
What I'm questioning is the conduct of the police.
He said that the Turkish Red Crescent would give advice on what constituted exceptional circumstances.

watt

COUNT NOUN

A **watt** is a unit of measuring electrical power.

. . . a 20 watt compact fluorescent 'low energy' light bulb.

---

where
wear, wears, wearing, wore, worn   /weə^r/
ware, wares

See also **war, wore; worn, warn**.

where

CONJUNCTION, PRONOUN, OR ADVERB

Where is a frequently used conjunction, pronoun, or adverb. You are probably familiar with the uses shown in the examples below. Look in a COBUILD dictionary if you need a fuller explanation of the uses of this word.

Where are they headed?
...the Rose Theatre where William Shakespeare wrote and performed some of his greatest plays.
This is where the potential for fraud comes in.
The danger is that his remarks could throw Anglo-German relations back to where they were earlier this year.
The country's parliament has often seemed to be seaching for a compromise where none appeared possible.

wear

VERB

The clothes that you **wear** are the clothes that you put on your body.

They only gave me a few old clothes to wear.
One wears black socks, the other wears white.

UNCOUNT NOUN

Wear is the use that things have over a period of time which causes damage to them.

Aircraft engineers use it because of its high strength and resistance to wear.

● **Wear** also occurs in the following phrasal verbs: **wear away; wear down; wear off; wear out.**

ware

UNCOUNT NOUN

Ware is used to refer to objects that are made of a particular substance or that are used for a particular purpose. When **ware** is used in this way, it is always modified.

...Waterford, the Irish luxury crystal ware maker.

PLURAL NOUN

Someone's **wares** are the things that they sell, usually in the street or in a market; an old-fashioned word.

The market traders started selling their wares at half-price.

---

whether
weather, weathers, weathering, weathered

/we̲ðə^r/

---

whether

CONJUNCTION

Whether is used to refer to a choice or doubt between two or more alternatives.

Over thirty studies have already been conducted to determine whether a link exists between coffee consumption and coronary heart disease.
Whether she could ever have beaten Tulu will never be known.

CONJUNCTION

Whether is used to say that something is true when either of two alternatives is the case.

Job cuts look inevitable at the company whether Hanson buys it or not.

weather

UNCOUNT NOUN

The **weather** is the condition of the atmosphere in an area at a particular time, for example, if it is raining, hot, or windy.

The weather can vary dramatically from place to place.
The ships were delayed for three days by bad weather.

VERB

If you **weather** a difficult time, you survive it.

The league has been through serious crises in the last 45 years, and it managed to weather these.

---

which
witch, witches

/wɪtʃ/

---

which

DETERMINER OR PRONOUN

Which is a frequently used determiner and pronoun. You are probably familiar with the uses shown in the examples below. Look in a COBUILD dictionary if you need a fuller explanation of the uses of this word.

I know one of us is going to die, I've just got to know which one.
The defence review which Mr King unveiled in the Commons on Wednesday is far-reaching in its scope.
It takes me an hour from door to door, which is not bad.

witch

COUNT NOUN

A **witch** is a woman who is believed to have magic powers.

In the 17th century she could have been burnt as a witch.

whole
hole, holes

/hoʊl/

whole

SINGULAR NOUN

The **whole** of something is all of it.

He said a stable Yugoslavia was important for the stability of the region and the whole of Europe.
The whole of the city centre was packed with demonstrators.

SINGULAR NOUN

A **whole** is a single thing containing several different parts. When **whole** is used in this way, it is usually modified.

The earth's weather system is an integrated whole.

ADJECTIVE

Whole is used to refer to all of something.

Some lectures and meals bring the whole community together.

ADJECTIVE

Something that is **whole** is undamaged or in one piece.

Fortunately, the plates were still whole.
The snake can swallow a small rat whole.

ADJECTIVE

You use **whole** to emphasize what you are saying; an informal use.

...a whole new way of life.
Charles was a whole lot nicer than I had expected.

hole

COUNT NOUN

A **hole** is an opening or a hollow space in something solid.

...a deep hole in the ground.
If you cut a hole in the center, the doughnut will cook faster.

whose
who's

/huːz/

whose

PRONOUN

Whose is used to indicate that something belongs or relates to a thing or person already mentioned.

*None was more admired than Adam Thorpe, whose 'Ulverton'
succeeded in evoking a long-gone rural England.*
*My son attends a prep school in London whose headmaster is called
Mr Pendleton.*

DETERMINER OR PRONOUN

Whose is used to ask about or refer to the person that something
belongs or relates to.

The paper asks whose side they are on.
Whose fault is that?

who's

Who's is the usual spoken form of 'who is'.

The lead vocalist Nancy, who's 16, is Dutch.
Nicolas, who's in Barbados, is undergoing tests for possible malaria.

Who's is the usual spoken form of 'who has'.

He's a water engineer who's been working in the Solomon Islands.

---

wield, wields, wielding, wielded
wheeled

/wiːld/

---

wield

VERB

If you **wield** a weapon, you carry it and use it.

He showed him how to wield a machete.

VERB

To **wield** power means to have it and be able to use it.

*That the new constitution has been approved by the Council is a
measure of the influence they still wield.*

wheeled

VERB

Wheeled is the '-ed' form of the verb 'wheel'. See **we'll, wheel, weal**
for an explanation of the uses of this word.

*It was in September 1940 that Hitler called operation Sealion off and
wheeled away eastwards towards Russia and destruction.*

wine, wines
whine, whines, whining, whined

/waɪn/

wine

MASS NOUN

Wine is an alcoholic drink which is usually made from grapes.

...low-alcohol fruit wines.
It is true that such wines are best served at room temperature.

whine

VERB

To **whine** about something means to complain about it, especially in an annoying way.

They whine about media neglect by the big television networks.
He whines about being a poor old man.

VERB

To **whine** means to make a long, high-pitched noise, especially one which sounds sad or unpleasant.

The dog began to whine to go out.

COUNT NOUN

A **whine** is a long, high-pitched noise, especially one which sounds sad or unpleasant.

She heard the children's cries and whines.

wither, withers, withering, withered
whither

/wɪðə^r/

wither

VERB

When things **wither**, they become weaker, often until they no longer exist.

...a tradition too cherished to be allowed to wither.

VERB

When plants **wither**, they shrink, dry up, and die.

The grass may wither in late summer.

whither

ADVERB OR CONJUNCTION

Whither means 'to which place'; an old-fashioned word.

The place to look would be in the West Country and Wales, whither the British were gradually pushed back.

---

won't
wont

/w**oo**nt/

---

won't

Won't is the usual spoken form of 'will not'.

They say they won't be satisfied until the building is back in the hands of the Greek Orthodox Church.
If the state won't give us the money, we will have to earn our own keep.

wont

ADJECTIVE

If someone is **wont** to do something, they do it regularly as a habit; an old-fashioned word.

Leo Tolstoy was wont to consider his life a failure.

---

wrap, wraps, wrapping, wrapped
rap, raps, rapping, rapped

/r**æ**p/

---

wrap

VERB

If you **wrap** something in, for example, paper or cloth, you put the paper or cloth round it so that it is completely covered.

Glover began to wrap the silver in tissue paper.
He wrapped himself in a bathrobe.

VERB

If you **wrap** something such as a piece of paper or cloth around something, you put it round it.

You are given a hot towel to wrap around yourself.
A handkerchief was wrapped around his left hand.

VERB

If you **wrap** your arms or fingers around something, you put them tightly around it.

He wrapped his arms around her.

● **Wrap** also occurs in the phrasal verb **wrap up**.

rap

VERB

If you **rap** on something, or if you **rap** it, you hit it with a series of quick blows.

Alex tapped on the window again, rapping the glass with the knuckles of his right hand.

COUNT NOUN

A **rap** is a quick hit or a knock on something.

There was a rap on her door. 'Yes?' she called irritably.

UNCOUNT NOUN

Rap is a style of pop music in which someone talks rhythmically to a musical background.

Rap is one of the most important developments in popular music in the past decade.

---

wreak, wreaks, wreaking, wreaked
reek, reeks, reeking, reeked

/riːk/

---

wreak

VERB

If something **wreaks** havoc or damage, it causes it.

These chemicals can wreak havoc on crops.
...the hurricane that wreaked havoc in the south of England.

VERB

To **wreak** revenge means to take revenge.

The army was wreaking a bloody vengeance upon the North.

reek

VERB

If someone or something **reeks of** a particular thing, they smell very strongly of it.

Parrish came in reeking of aftershave lotion.
The apartment reeked of pizza.

COUNT NOUN

A **reek of** something is a very strong smell of it.

He smelt the reek of whisky.

---

wretch, wretches   /retʃ/
retch, retches, retching, retched

---

wretch

COUNT NOUN

You can refer to someone who is wicked or unfortunate as a **wretch**; a literary word.

A country priest is only a poor wretch like other men.

retch

VERB

If you **retch**, your stomach moves and you make a sound as if you were going to be sick.

The smell made me retch.

---

wrote
rote   /rout/

---

wrote

Wrote is the past tense form of the verb 'write'. See **right, write, rite** for an explanation of the uses of this word.

Amy opened her handbag and took out a piece of paper. She wrote on it her name and the hostel address.
When I was in high school, I wrote an essay on what kind of mother I wanted to be when I grew up.

rote

ADJECTIVE

If you learn something **by rote**, you learn it by memorizing it rather than by understanding it.

He had learned to spell by rote without really understanding the rules.

wry
rye
/raɪ/

wry

ADJECTIVE

If someone has a **wry** expression, it shows that they find a bad or difficult situation slightly amusing or ironic.

She said this with a wry glance at me.

ADJECTIVE

A **wry** remark or piece of writing refers to a bad or difficult situation in an amusing or ironic way.

The book is a wry comment on the way that Britain dealt with bright people such as Clarke after the Second World War.

rye

UNCOUNT NOUN

Rye is a type of cereal grass that is grown in cold countries to make food for animals and some types of bread and whisky.

It produces far more rye and barley than the United States.

---

yolk, yolks
yoke, yokes
/joʊk/

yolk

VARIABLE NOUN

The **yolk** of an egg is the yellow part in the middle of it.

Make a mayonnaise with the egg yolk and oil.
Beat the cream and egg yolks together in a bowl.

yoke

SINGULAR NOUN

If you say that people are under the **yoke** of a bad thing or person, you mean that they are in a difficult or unhappy state because of that thing or person; a literary use.

People are still suffering under the yoke of slavery.
The colonial yoke brought some industrialisation and modern education.

COUNT NOUN

A **yoke** is a long piece of wood tied across the necks of two animals in order to make them walk close together when they are pulling a plough.

The wooden yoke chafes the oxen's necks.

you
yew, yews
ewe, ewes

/juː/

See also **use, yews, ewes**.

you

PRONOUN

A speaker or writer uses **you** to refer to the person or people he or she is speaking to.

What do you think of this?
Would you like a cup of tea or coffee?

PRONOUN

You is also used to refer to people in general rather than to a particular person or group.

You can get freezers with security locks.
You can make 6 per cent interest putting money in the bank.

yew

COUNT NOUN

A **yew** is a type of tree.

...yew hedges.
...Crathes Castle, famous for the beauty of its great yews.

ewe

COUNT NOUN

A **ewe** is a female sheep.

A flock of 700 ewes produces 900 lambs a year.

your
yore

/jɔːʳ/

your

DETERMINER

Your is used to indicate that something belongs or relates to the person or people someone is speaking to.

You can pick up your mail there too.
By all means make your own decision.
She said you'd make a mess of your life and you have.

DETERMINER

Your is used to indicate that something belongs or relates to people in general rather than to a particular person or group.

Stress is when pressure exceeds your ability to cope.
A powerful stream of X-rays can shine right through your hand.

yore

PHRASE

The expression **of yore** is used to refer to a period of time long ago; an old-fashioned expression.

...the heaven of the gods of yore.

Index

If the word you are looking for is the first word in an entry, it appears on its own in **bold**. If it is not the first word in an entry, or if it is an inflected form of a word, it is followed by the symbol ⇨ and the word which does come first.

ad ⇨ **add**
aide ⇨ **aid**
ail ⇨ **ale**
air
aisle ⇨ **isle**
ale
allowed
alms ⇨ **arms**
aloud ⇨ **allowed**
altar ⇨ **alter**
alter
arc
Ark ⇨ **arc**
arms
ascent
assent ⇨ **ascent**
aye ⇨ **I**
bail
baize ⇨ **bays**
bald
bale ⇨ **bail**
ball
balmy ⇨ **barmy**
band
banned ⇨ **band**
banns ⇨ **bans**
bans
bare ⇨ **bear**
barer ⇨ **bearer**
baring ⇨ **bearing**
barmy
baron
barren ⇨ **baron**
base
bass ⇨ **base**
bawl ⇨ **ball**
bawled ⇨ **bald**
bays
be
beach
bear

bearer
bearing
beat
bee ⇨ **be**
beech ⇨ **beach**
beet ⇨ **beat**
bell
belle ⇨ **bell**
berry ⇨ **bury**
berth ⇨ **birth**
billed ⇨ **build**
birth
bite
blew ⇨ **blue**
bloc ⇨ **block**
block
blue
boar ⇨ **bore**
board ⇨ **bored**
bode ⇨ **bowed**
bold
bolder
bore
bored
born
borne ⇨ **born**
bough ⇨ **bow**
boulder ⇨ **bolder**
bow
bowed
bowled ⇨ **bold**
boy
brake ⇨ **break**
bread
break
bred ⇨ **bread**
brewed
brews
bridal ⇨ **bridle**
bridle
broach ⇨ **brooch**

brooch
brood ⇨ **brewed**
brows ⇨ **browse**
browse
bruise ⇨ **brews**
build
buoy ⇨ **boy**
burger
burgher ⇨ **burger**
bury
bussed ⇨ **bust**
bust
buy ⇨ **by**
by
bye ⇨ **by**
byte ⇨ **bite**
cache ⇨ **cash**
calve ⇨ **carve**
calves ⇨ **carve**
cannon
canon ⇨ **cannon**
canvas
canvass ⇨ **canvas**
carat ⇨ **carrot**
carrot
carve
carves
cash
cast
caste ⇨ **cast**
caught ⇨ **court**
cause
cede ⇨ **seed**
ceiling
cell ⇨ **sell**
cellar ⇨ **seller**
censor ⇨ **sensor**
cent ⇨ **sent**
cereal
chased
chaste ⇨ **chased**
check
cheque ⇨ **check**
chews ⇨ **choose**
chilli
chilly ⇨ **chilli**
choose
chord ⇨ **cord**

chute ⇨ **shoot**
cite ⇨ **sight**
cited ⇨ **sighted**
clause
claws ⇨ **clause**
climb
clime ⇨ **climb**
coarse ⇨ **course**
colonel
complement ⇨ **compliment**
complementary ⇨ **complimentary**
compliment
complimentary
conker ⇨ **conquer**
conquer
coo ⇨ **coup**
cord
core
cores ⇨ **cause**
cornflour
cornflower ⇨ **cornflour**
corps ⇨ **core**
council
councillor
counsel ⇨ **council**
counsellor ⇨ **councillor**
coup
course
court
coward
cowered ⇨ **coward**
creak
creek ⇨ **creak**
crews ⇨ **cruise**
cruise
curb
currant ⇨ **current**
current
cymbal ⇨ **symbol**
dam ⇨ **damn**
damn
days
daze ⇨ **days**
dear
deer ⇨ **dear**
desert
dessert ⇨ **desert**
dew ⇨ **due**

die
disc
discreet
discrete ⇨ discreet
disk ⇨ disc
doe ⇨ dough
dough
draft
draught ⇨ draft
draw
drawer ⇨ draw
dual
due
duel ⇨ dual
dye ⇨ die
earn
elicit ⇨ illicit
ere ⇨ air
ewe ⇨ you
ewes ⇨ use
eye ⇨ I
fête ⇨ fate
fêted ⇨ fated
faint
fair
fare ⇨ fair
farther ⇨ father
fate
fated
father
faze ⇨ phase
feat ⇨ feet
feet
feint ⇨ faint
find
fined ⇨ find
fir ⇨ fur
flair
flare ⇨ flair
flaw ⇨ floor
flawed
flea ⇨ flee
flee
flew
floe ⇨ flow
floor
floored ⇨ flawed
flour ⇨ flower

flow
flower
flu ⇨ flew
flue ⇨ flew
for
fore ⇨ for
fort ⇨ fought
forth ⇨ fourth
fought
foul
four ⇨ for
fourth
fowl ⇨ foul
frees ⇨ freeze
freeze
frieze ⇨ freeze
fur
gait ⇨ gate
gamble
gambol ⇨ gamble
gate
geezer ⇨ geyser
geyser
gild ⇨ guild
gilt ⇨ guilt
gnaw ⇨ nor
gorilla ⇨ guerrilla
grate ⇨ great
grater ⇨ greater
great
greater
grill
grille ⇨ grill
grisly
grizzly ⇨ grisly
groan ⇨ grown
grown
guerrilla
guessed ⇨ guest
guest
guild
guilt
hail
hair
hale ⇨ hail
hall
hangar
hanger ⇨ hangar

hare ⇨ hair
haul ⇨ hall
hay ⇨ hey
heal
hear ⇨ here
heard
hears ⇨ here's
heel ⇨ heal
heir ⇨ air
herd ⇨ heard
here's
here
heroin
heroine ⇨ heroin
hew ⇨ hue
hey
hi ⇨ high
high
him
hoard
hoarse ⇨ horse
hole ⇨ whole
horde ⇨ hoard
horse
hour ⇨ our
hours ⇨ ours
hue
hymn ⇨ him
I
idle
idol ⇨ idle
illicit
in
inn ⇨ in
invade
inveighed ⇨ invade
isle
jam
jamb ⇨ jam
kerb ⇨ curb
kernel ⇨ colonel
key
knead ⇨ need
knew ⇨ new
knight ⇨ night
knit
knot ⇨ not
know ⇨ no

knows
lain ⇨ lane
lane
laps
lapse ⇨ laps
larva ⇨ lava
laud ⇨ lord
lava
law
lays
laze ⇨ lays
lead ⇨ led
leak
leant ⇨ lent
leased ⇨ least
least
led
leek ⇨ leak
lent
lessen ⇨ lesson
lesson
licence
license ⇨ licence
lichen ⇨ liken
lightening ⇨ lightning
lightning
liken
links
loan
lone ⇨ loan
loot
lord
lore ⇨ law
lute ⇨ loot
lynx ⇨ links
made
maid ⇨ made
mail ⇨ male
main
maize
male
mane ⇨ main
manner
manor ⇨ manner
mare ⇨ mayor
marshal
martial ⇨ marshal
mat

matt ⇨ **mat**
mayor
maze ⇨ **maize**
mean
meat ⇨ **meet**
medal
meddle ⇨ **medal**
meet
metal
mettle ⇨ **metal**
mews ⇨ **muse**
mien ⇨ **mean**
mind
mined ⇨ **mind**
miner
minor ⇨ **miner**
missed
mist ⇨ **missed**
moan
mode
moose ⇨ **mousse**
morning
mourning ⇨ **morning**
mousse
mowed ⇨ **mode**
mown ⇨ **moan**
muscle
muse
mussel ⇨ **muscle**
need
new
night
nit ⇨ **knit**
no
nor
nose ⇨ **knows**
not
oar ⇨ **or**
or
ore ⇨ **or**
our
ours
overseas
oversees ⇨ **overseas**
paced ⇨ **paste**
pail ⇨ **pale**
pain
pair

palate
pale
palette ⇨ **palate**
pallet ⇨ **palate**
panda
pander ⇨ **panda**
pane ⇨ **pain**
par ⇨ **pair**
passed ⇨ **past**
past
paste
pastel
pastille ⇨ **pastel**
pause
paw ⇨ **pour**
pawn
paws ⇨ **pause**
peace
peak
peal ⇨ **peel**
pear ⇨ **pair**
pedal
peddle ⇨ **pedal**
peek ⇨ **peak**
peel
peer
pervade
phase
pidgin ⇨ **pigeon**
piece ⇨ **peace**
pier ⇨ **peer**
pigeon
pique ⇨ **peak**
place
plaice ⇨ **place**
plain ⇨ **plane**
plane
pleas ⇨ **please**
please
plum
plumb ⇨ **plum**
pole ⇨ **poll**
poll
poor ⇨ **pour**
populace ⇨ **populous**
populous
pore ⇨ **pour**
pores ⇨ **pause**

porn ⇨ **pawn**
pour
pours ⇨ **pause**
practice
practise ⇨ **practice**
praise
pray
prays ⇨ **praise**
prey ⇨ **pray**
preys ⇨ **praise**
principal ⇨ **principle**
principle
prise ⇨ **prize**
prize
profit
program ⇨ **programme**
programme
prophet ⇨ **profit**
purveyed ⇨ **pervade**
quay ⇨ **key**
rap ⇨ **wrap**
read
red ⇨ **read**
reed ⇨ **read**
reek ⇨ **wreak**
rest
retch ⇨ **wretch**
review
revive ⇨ **review**
right
ring
rite ⇨ **right**
road
rode ⇨ **road**
roll
role ⇨ **roll**
rose
rota
rotor ⇨ **rota**
root
rote ⇨ **wrote**
rough
rouse ⇨ **rows**
route ⇨ **root**
rows
rung
rye ⇨ **wry**
sac ⇨ **sack**

sack
sail ⇨ **sale**
sale
sauce ⇨ **source**
saw
scene ⇨ **seen**
scent ⇨ **sent**
sea ⇨ **see**
sealing ⇨ **ceiling**
seam ⇨ **seem**
seas ⇨ **sees**
see
seed
seem
seen
sees
seize ⇨ **sees**
sell
seller
sensor
sent
serf ⇨ **surf**
serial ⇨ **cereal**
sew ⇨ **so**
shake
shear ⇨ **sheer**
sheer
sheikh ⇨ **shake**
shoe
shoo ⇨ **shoe**
shoot
side
sighed ⇨ **side**
sighs ⇨ **size**
sight
sighted
site ⇨ **sight**
sited ⇨ **sighted**
size
slay ⇨ **sleigh**
sleigh
so
soar
sole ⇨ **soul**
some
son
sore ⇨ **soar**
sort

sought ⇨ **sort**
soul
source
sow ⇨ **so**
staid ⇨ **stayed**
stair
stake
stalk
stare ⇨ **stair**
stationary ⇨ **stationery**
stationery
stayed
steak ⇨ **stake**
steal
steel ⇨ **steal**
stile ⇨ **style**
storey ⇨ **story**
stork ⇨ **stalk**
story
straight
straightened
strait ⇨ **straight**
straitened ⇨ **straightened**
style
suede ⇨ **swayed**
suite ⇨ **sweet**
sum ⇨ **some**
sun ⇨ **son**
swayed
sweet
symbol
tail ⇨ **tale**
tale
taught
taut ⇨ **taught**
tea
team
tear
teas ⇨ **tea**
tee ⇨ **tea**
teem ⇨ **team**
tees ⇨ **tea**
the
thee ⇨ **the**
their
theirs
there ⇨ **their**
there's ⇨ **theirs**

threw ⇨ **through**
throes ⇨ **throws**
throne ⇨ **thrown**
through
thrown
throws
thyme ⇨ **time**
tic ⇨ **tick**
tick
tide ⇨ **tied**
tied
tier ⇨ **tear**
time
tire
to
toe
ton
tonne ⇨ **ton**
too ⇨ **to**
tow ⇨ **toe**
troop
troupe ⇨ **troop**
tuba ⇨ **tuber**
tuber
two ⇨ **to**
tyre ⇨ **tire**
urn ⇨ **earn**
use
vain
vale ⇨ **veil**
vane ⇨ **vain**
veil
vein ⇨ **vain**
wade ⇨ **weighed**
wail ⇨ **whale**
wailing ⇨ **whaling**
waist ⇨ **waste**
wait
waited
waive ⇨ **wave**
war
ware ⇨ **where**
warn
waste
watt ⇨ **what**
wave
way
we've

239

weak ⇨ **week**
weal ⇨ **we'll**
wear ⇨ **where**
weather ⇨ **whether**
weave ⇨ **we've**
week
weigh ⇨ **way**
weighed
weight ⇨ **wait**
weighted ⇨ **waited**
we'll
wet
whale
whaling
what
wheel ⇨ **we'll**
wheeled ⇨ **wield**
where
whet ⇨ **wet**
whether
whey ⇨ **way**
which
whine ⇨ **wine**
whither ⇨ **wither**
who's ⇨ **whose**

whole
whose
wield
wine
witch ⇨ **which**
wither
won't
wont ⇨ **won't**
wore ⇨ **war**
worn ⇨ **warn**
wrap
wreak
unrest ⇨ **rest**
wretch
wring ⇨ **ring**
wrote
wrung ⇨ **rung**
wry
yew ⇨ **you**
yews ⇨ **use**
yoke ⇨ **yolk**
yolk
yore ⇨ **your**
you
your